W9-AGM-402

The Messiah Comes Tomorrow

Books by Alan Lupo

Rites-of-Way: The Politics of Transportation in Boston and the U.S. City 1971 (with Frank Colcord and Edmund Fowler)

Liberty's Chosen Home: The Politics of Violence in Boston 1977, 1988

For Better, For Worse 1979 (with Caryl Rivers)

The
Messiah
Comes
Tomorrow

TALES FROM THE AMERICAN SHTETL

ALAN LUPO

University of Massachusetts Press • *Amherst*

Sources and acknowledgments for the pieces included in this book appear on
the last pages.
LC 00-030276
ISBN 1-55849-283-6
Designed by Jack Harrison
Set in ITC Cheltenham by Graphic Composition, Inc.
Printed and bound by Thomson-Shore, Inc.

Library of Congress Cataloging-in-Publication Data
Lupo, Alan.
   The Messiah comes tomorrow : tales from the American shtetl / Alan Lupo.
      p. cm.
   ISBN 1-55849-283-6 (alk. paper)
   1. Jews—Massachusetts—Boston—Social life and customs.
2. Jews—Massachusetts—Boston—Biography. 3. Lupo, Alan.   I. Title.
F73.9.J5 L86 2000
974.4′61004924—dc21

                                                    00-030276

This book is published with the support and cooperation of the University of
Massachusetts Boston.

To my *mishpocheh,* Caryl, Steve, Alyssa, Connie, Ogie, and Lauren, with all my love.

To those characters whose very lives supplied the rhythm and cadence of these humble offerings.

To Carolyn Toll Oppenheim, a journalist and *landsman,* who convinced me that this book was possible and the right thing to do.

CONTENTS

INTRODUCTION   Good Old Days, and Not So Good   1

CHAPTER ONE   *Mishpocheh* and *Machetunim:* Family and
    Yet More Family   11

Grandma's Favorite Warning   13
The Messiah Comes Tomorrow   16
A Stroll through the Old Neighborhood   22
Comforting New Generations   25
Memories of Max   28
A House and Its Memories   31
Thanks, but It's Too Late   34
On Christmas Eve, a Toast to Two Who Cared   37
The Continuity of Family   40

CHAPTER TWO   Comfortable? It's a Living   43

Where a Sigh Can Speak Volumes   45
Drucker, Murder, Inc., Hoodlum, Dies in Prison   50
Used Clothing Store Brings "Block" Madison Ave. Pitch   53
Burlesque Comedian Reminisces about Early Days—and
    the Changes   55
A Bad Bet   58
Sticking by the Union   61

CHAPTER THREE   What Ever Happened to National
    Brotherhood Week? Wait . . . It Breathes Yet   65

Diversity: So What's the Problem?   67
The Jewish Defense League   70
Today I Am a Fountain Penski   82
From Russia with Hate   85
Is There a Double Standard for Jews?   89
Those Who Judge Israel   92

CHAPTER FOUR   The Good Old Days Are Now—Well,
    Mostly   95

Ahead of Her Time for Going On-Line   97
Acting to Make Parents Proud   99

My Son the Cop   102
Noblesse Obliges Him to Forgo the Throne   105
Kasha *Varnishkes* à la Academy of Holy Names   108
A Couple of Shots of Blended   111

CHAPTER FIVE   Hello, God, I Haven't Forgotten You,
    Especially as I Age   115
The Saving of a Shul   117
No Heat, but Much Light   120
Remembering Nine Good Men, and One Boy, Who Knew
    How to Pray   122
Praying for Compassion   125

SOURCES AND ACKNOWLEDGMENTS   129

The Messiah Comes Tomorrow

Good Old Days,
and Not So Good

One day, while reading with some disgust how families were spending thousands of dollars for their children's bar and bat mitzvahs, I recalled my own transition into manhood in 1951.

That was a pretty good year for my friends and me, because Sid Gordon ended up with 29 home runs and a batting average of .287. Gordon had come to the Boston Braves at the end of the 1949 season from the New York Giants. The Braves, unlike the vaunted Red Sox, were considered the workingman's team. They had what we now call diversity, including even a black outfielder, Sam Jethroe. Gordon was an outfielder and a third baseman. More important to my crowd, he was Jewish.

I suppose that, by 1951, there were Jewish families who felt totally secure in America. I imagine they were mostly German Jewish folks. Most of us were insecure. We still were not convinced of how solid our footing was. We knew that many were the times when we, as a people, had felt welcomed in one place or another and, then, suddenly, maybe the economy soured, and guess who got the not-so-flat end of the sword?

Also, at about that time, we were witnessing a resurgence of anti-Semitism. The word on the street among the bigots was that Jewish guys really had not fought in World War II, that Jews were chicken, that Jews were cheap, that Jews were commies, that Jews were capitalists bent on world, or, at least, U.S. control.

How we got to be commies and super-capitalists at the same time has befuddled me to this day, when, by the way, we are witnessing yet another resurgence, the theme of which seems to be that we Jews are part of ZOG, or Zionist Occupied Government. Well, at this stage of the game, it's okay by me. I should like to put in my application to be Secretary of the Treasury. If we are going to be in charge, I want to handle the dough and make one final, big score.

Back in 1951, however, we were not laughing at the bigotry. We were looking over our shoulders, watching our flanks and, at times, traveling in packs. We had learned from fathers and older brothers that Jews not only could fight back, but had to. It was nice to honor those learned in the ways of the talmud; it was also nice, maybe crucial, to honor the *shtarkers,* the tough guys. So, defensively, we learned the lore of both criminals and sports figures.

Therefore, the arrival in 1950 of Sidney Gordon, a Brooklyn boy, a right-handed power hitter standing at five feet, ten inches and weighing in at 185 pounds, was a seminal moment for both kids and adults who craved heroes. No visiting rabbi, no hero from the young state of Israel, in short, nobody else could have caused the stir of affection.

In what was clearly an act defying the stereotypes that women were uninterested in sports, one girl I knew kept Sid Gordon's 1950 Bowman baseball card in her wallet. By 1951, he was probably more worn out from appearing at "Father-Son" temple breakfasts than by patrolling old Braves Field.

That year, though I was so nervous as to be ill, I performed somewhat credibly at my bar mitzvah, making no mistakes, as I recall, and was given a prayer book with my name inscribed on it and misspelled. In those days of PFS, pre fancy-shmancy, we had a buffet lunch in the gym of the Winthrop, Massachusetts Jewish Community Center on Shirley Street, which was then the ghetto shopping area for the urban community's large Jewish population.

I ate well of the chopped liver and herring and got lots of U.S. savings bonds. That night, I went to bed before our relatives left our small apartment. They stayed and played gin rummy. I fell asleep with their raucous conversation and laughter echoing in my ears.

What more, I wondered as I read recently of the ostentatious displays of wealth, does one need? Perhaps one needs to be reminded that what is reality now was quite different once. Indeed, if history is truly more than the recounting of larger-than-life figures engaged in grand events, then to write of the joys and tragedies of common people is crucial for us all to understand ourselves.

In 1968, after living elsewhere in the country for about a decade, I moved back to the community where I had grown up, and now I occasionally drive or walk through what was that shoppers' ghetto. Once, there were three kosher meat markets. Now, there are none. Once there was a deli offering what locals said was the best hot corned beef on a bulkie roll this side of New York. Long gone. The Roosevelt Beauty Salon is gone, as is the Roosevelt Credit Union. We were very big on FDR. Kaplow's Creamery, run by the very family who were our downstairs landlords, is but a memory. The Jewish Community Center remains, but only as a building, not as a Jewish anything. A memorial to two local Jewish guys who died in World War II stands on a corner as a lonely reminder of what was once a bustling, noisy, Jewish working-stiff neighborhood. Those two men, Levy and Bramson, frozen forever in their youth, are the ghosts that haunt what was.

Except for the Hasidic communities, gone with the death of my grandparents, parents and their generations and disappearing with the upward mobility of mine and subsequent generations is the poetry of a people: the know-it-all corner talk of local wise guys; the Yiddish-accented English of the Russian and European immigrants; the leftover Yiddish curses and blessings and the inherited shrugs and singsong patter of their American-born offspring and grandkids.

Gone too is the time of folktales, when a grandmother or uncle would hold forth in the parlor or kitchen about some relative or incident in another country. The tales, real and apocryphal, became litany, repeated and recited by subsequent generations until television arrived and replaced the spoken word and the piano sing-alongs.

In that time there were as many Jewish salesmen, carpenters, glaziers, butchers, milkmen, and bartenders as there were lawyers, doctors, and accountants.

For too long now, the perception of Jews in America is that of an upper-middle-class people engaged mainly in "the professions" and rarely doing the dirty work. For much too long, thanks to the clichés of modern literature and film, the Jew is seen as a *kvetch,* a whining, self-pitying, mother-resenting character.

Lost, somehow, are the others—the working stiffs, the small-time business owners, the amateur scholars, the bookies, and street sluggers. They deserve their shot. Generations of readers born after World War II should understand what once predominated and what sometimes can still be found. Such characters—very few of them famous—are part of the rich American landscape.

My father Max grew up with Jewish guys named Soapy and Spongy. I grew up with Jewish guys named Klotzer, Izzy, Rosie, Tiny, Monk, The Penguin, Butch, Sammy, Rocky, and The Heap.

Had I included in this book, this small piece of history and folklore, this modest testimonial to a people and their time, only the stories and columns of personal and family recollections, I could have been at ease with my conscience that I had fulfilled the task I set for myself.

But my four decades as a journalist enabled me to meet and write about others, about people who were strangers to me until we began talking, until I was able to write about them. Then, I felt I had known them in my soul as well as I had known my family and those guys with whom I had grown up. It was if I had carried the seed of their experiences, just as I feel I am the repository of all that preceded me.

This is, of course, somewhat presumptuous. Who am I to take on such a rich history?

I am the sole offspring of Esther Sacon and Max Lupo, both of blessed memory. She was one of four children born to Barnett and Rose Sacon, formerly Saconovitz and formerly of Minsk. He was one of five born to Kate and Isaac Lupo, formerly Lupescu, she maybe from Minsk too, and he, from Romania. In both families, the men left their wives. Both families struggled. My father was the only one of four brothers who graduated from high school. Were these the "good old days" to which ahistoric observers are forever referring?

My mother's brother, my father, and two of his brothers became salesmen. His youngest brother, standing over six feet, four inches, had an operatic voice and became a singing bartender.

I describe some of their lives in a few of the stories and columns, but those who already have read these offerings say I must also describe myself. I suppose the consumer has a right to know, what with truth-in-packaging.

As I write these words, I am 61, a reporter and columnist for the *Boston Globe*. I have been fortunate enough to have written some books and to have done television and radio, but it is in newsprint where my soul resides. I have been a journalist for more than two-thirds of those 61 years. When I started out, there were more big-city newspapers than there are today, and they were peopled mainly by white guys who wore white shirts, often stained, and wrinkled, ugly ties, and sometimes, yes, fedora hats—even indoors. They rolled up the sleeves of their white shirts and worked with ink, paste, and dirty newsprint.

They came from the working-stiff neighborhoods and often remained there, so they were bigshots in their own little worlds. Many of them never set foot on a college campus, but the readers felt connected to them. Would that they did today.

We typed our stories on cheap paper with carbon copies and on old, black Underwoods or Royals or Coronas. We made chump change for money, and some of us drank too much and stayed out too late.

Today, our attire is varied, as is the ethnic and racial makeup of our newsrooms. More women than men enter our profession, which we used to call a racket or a game. We are more educated and less street-smart. We are more thoughtful and less poetic in our speech. Our writing is more sophisticated and informed. We probably do a better job than we used to, but we wonder if it's all too late, as the public seems intent on dumbing itself down on televised and Internet fare.

For many years, Jews gravitated toward journalism. Some theorize it is because we are allegedly "the people of the book." I respect that, but I also respect the people who made book. But I'll let the stories in this book speak to that.

There were, despite our proclivity to report and write and edit, newspapers where Jews were a small minority. From 1962 through most of 1966, I worked for the *Baltimore Evening Sun,* now also of blessed memory. One day, a Jewish cabbie dropped me off near the loading dock at the back of the newspaper plant.

"So, you work here?" he asked.

I confirmed that.

"So, what do you do? You work on the loading dock, what?"

"I'm a reporter."

He turned in disbelief. "Naw, get outta here. A reporter?"

"What's the big deal? Jews can't be reporters?" I said, laughing.

"Not there," he said, not laughing.

"Bullshit," I responded.

"Yeah? Look around when you get back in there."

I got back in there and looked around. He was right. There weren't many of us. I never inferred that that was the result of any anti-Semitism. It's just the way it was on some papers. So, consciously or otherwise, I found myself doing more than a few feature stories about Jews. They included characters who worked The Block, which was actually about three or four city blocks of strip joints, bars and secondhand retail joints.

Those people reminded me—as if I needed reminding—of those with whom I had grown up, of those in my ΑΕΠ fraternity house at the University of Massachusetts in Amherst in the late 1950s, of those I had met and covered in the Catskills of Sullivan County, New York, on my first newspaper, the *Middletown Times-Herald Record,* in 1961 and 1962.

I began to realize, perhaps subconsciously, that I had no choice but to be a repository of all those people and their stories. I had, after all, spent much time in my youth with Rose Sacon, my mother's mother. She was my most loyal supporter, my most trustworthy ally, my best friend. She spoke to me in Yiddish and heavily accented English. She told me stories and loved me without reservation.

When I married my Columbia University journalism school classmate Caryl Rivers, then of Silver Spring, Maryland, a graduate of St. Michael's, Academy of the Holy Names, and Trinity College, I found my nana's Irish clone in Mamie Mangan Rivers, Caryl's paternal grandmother, who lived across the street from Caryl and who loved that lovable kid without reservation.

Our intentions to marry in 1962 caused some stir among

family, especially my parents. I understood some of their fear. I had, after all, grown up in their world. But my generation was perhaps a bridge to a different America, a more diverse nation, in which differences were becoming more acceptable, a place where it mattered less to Italian parents that a son of Naples might marry a daughter of Milan, or to Irish parents, that a daughter of County Clare should marry a son of Warsaw.

We were married by a Reform rabbi. Our families embraced and got along as if they had known one another for a half century. Caryl and I agreed to try to raise the kids as Jews. There are those who would deny our right to do this, for the mother was raised Catholic and has seen no need to deny her upbringing, and neither of us has seen any need for her to formally convert.

Our son Steve and our daughter Alyssa regard themselves as Jews. Like their parents, they have little or no truck with the rules and regulations of various organized religions. He is a police officer in Texas, and she is an actor and teacher in California.

Our daughter-in-law, Connie, a Protestant raised in Nebraska, seems to have cornered the market on menorahs; I buy her cassettes of klezmer music. The *ketubah,* or wedding contract, is framed and hangs in their living room. Our granddaughter Lauren volunteered Steve to lecture the Bear Creek Elementary School kids in Euless, Texas, on Chanukah. "He did real good," she reported. Our daughter and Ogie, her fiancé, a Filipino American, have a mezuzah on their doorjamb. They and their friends celebrate Pesach seders. She and I do Yiddish accents together. They all lead moral lives, and they have done more than their share of good deeds. They, as their mother and I, have friends of all races, creeds, and ethnic backgrounds. It is the American *mitzvah*—a good work.

For my part, I talk to them often about Jews, about our history, about our traditions of learning, charity, and family. I stress that we have a special obligation to survive, given the sacrifices of those denied that basic right. And, yes, I talk to them of Sid Gordon. Unlike their father, however, they feel no need to check the box scores for Jewish names.

They are more secure as Americans than I was or am. This was inevitable, but I do not want them to forget the folk tales, the accents, the attitudes, the humor, the pathos of Jews. So, then, I become a self-appointed repository.

Though I know little of who my people were in Minsk and Bukovina, though I can only guess at their fate for not having emigrated, it is as if I know them and can sing their songs and tell their little jokes.

It is, then, to them too that I wish to dedicate this collection of stories and columns, for whatever the subjects of these stories said, did, felt, it sprang from the life force of those who may not have survived the Cossack, the Stalinist, the Iron Guard, the Nazi.

What follows are real stories about real people. None of it is fiction. All of it was written on deadline for the various publishers who, defying their own common sense, kept me for a time on their payrolls.

The aging burlesque comedian, the bookie who swore he wouldn't rat on his Mob associates, the dealer of secondhand clothing, the aunt and uncle who would never move to a promised apartment, all deserve better than to be preserved in some yellowing newsclips that will deteriorate with age and fall apart, as if to signify that such people never even existed.

CHAPTER ONE

Mishpocheh and *Machetunim:* Family and Yet More Family

In the 1940s and into the next decade, my friends and I lived in a neatly circumscribed world, an often comfortable place that would soon fall apart in the face of automobile ownership, television sets, the interstate highways, and suburbia. We knew what we knew. We knew our block, our school, our families, our daily habits.

Life on Tewksbury Street and its accompanying streets of mixed-income housing had its predictable patterns. In the mornings, my mother ate a bulkie roll and drank a cup of coffee while reading the *Boston Post.* In the evening, my father took the subway from Boston to Maverick Station in East Boston, where he picked up a bus that let him off four blocks from our street, and I would wait for him on the corner. He carried the *Boston Traveler,* an afternoon paper.

Meals were pretty much at the same time each day. There was no dinner. There was supper. Bedtime was rarely to be trifled with, though an exception was made once weekly to enable some of us to listen—from our beds, of course—to "The Lone Ranger" on radio.

We had not learned yet that many parents didn't get along or even know how to begin to do so. We had not yet been subjected to the byzantine politics, indeed, the internecine warfare that mark the life cycles of many families.

Family was Esther and Max up the stairs, and Nana who would visit from Brookline. It was Uncle Leo and Aunt

Francis and cousins Marlene and Bonnie a dozen streets away. It was Aunt Dorothy and Uncle Bob, in uniform, dropping in. It was Uncle Nadie and Aunt Yetta and their kids Lennie and Stanley in the three-decker not far from the trolley line in Boston's Mattapan neighborhood. Just about everyone on both sides of our family lived and worked within striking distance of subways and trolleys. They were *mishpocheh.* You could depend on them. You knew their walks, their accents, their peculiar individual shrugs and lamentations.

Only later, as you and cousins married, did you learn that family could exist not only near the subway, but across the continent. Then, you knew of *machetunim,* in-laws, and extended family. Given that we all begin with families, long before we meet up with friends, enemies, bosses, competitors, admirers, and detractors, it is only right that the first chapter of this collection is about family, the good and the not-so-good.

Grandma's Favorite Warning

We had heard all the warnings as kids. You stand in the rain, you'll get a chill, you'll get sick. You don't look both ways, you'll get hit by a car, don't come running home crying to me. You don't eat what's on your plate, I'll call a policeman, you'll get arrested.

You never heard this last one? Sure. While I picked at my food, my grandmother would tell me stories about rotten kids who refused to eat until the coppers came around and convinced them otherwise. She came from czarist Russia, where you could get arrested for looking at somebody the wrong way, so what was there not to believe?

We outgrew the food/cop story and tried to ignore the other warnings, but there was one fast shot high above the belt that takes a long time to go away:

"You could take out an eye!"

There is no threat, no promise or retribution, no suggestion of anything horrendous that came close to impressing those of us who heard these words.

To "take out an eye" did not mean to withdraw one from the eye bank. It did not mean that you personally were going to voluntarily remove an eye. It meant that you stood a very good chance of losing one. It was a Jewish-American phrase, the variation of which was, "You could take out an eye, yet."

The warning generally came at the end of a long, impassioned soliloquy by one's mother, grandmother, or even neighbor regarding some activity that she preferred you did not do.

Like tackle football on the street. Tackle football on the street was not one of my favorites, as I was too often the one tackled. But even if you were the tackler, it was no day at the beach. When anyone suggested, "You play that, you could fall on your head, and you could take out an eye," I was the first to exercise my free-agent clause and sit out the season. But the corneal countermand was not always reserved for such obvious potential trauma as might occur when someone knocked your face into a pothole.

Baseball is a good example. A kid would leave the apartment with a baseball, wrapped in black tape, a fielder's mitt and a wad of bubble gum attached to the inside of his right cheek.

"You're going out?" the grandmother would ask.

"No, I'm staying in," the kid would answer. No disrespect: it's just the way we talk to one another.

"So, where are you going all of a sudden?" she would persist.

"Hebrew school," he would say.

"You're playing that game where they throw the ball at you?"

He would groan.

"You'll be filthy dirty when you get home."

More groaning.

"They could hit you in the head, God forbid, with that ball."

Intense groaning, surrounding the phrase, "Aw, fah cryin' out loud."

The kid would be almost out the door. She knew she was losing him, she had one last shot:

"You could take out an eye, yet!"

He'd be out the door, but that warning would follow him down the stairs, out onto the street and all the way to the park. A ground ball, you can field. But how do you field the admonition that if you play shortstop, there is a very good chance you are going to come home looking like Moshe Dayan?

Three or four years ago, I was having lunch and reminiscing with Eddie, a boyhood pal whom I had not seen for too long a time. For years, into his thirties, Eddie said laughing, he used to walk down the street, looking over his shoulder. Too many warnings can make one a bit insecure.

"I was afraid," he said, "that when I looked, I'd see all these one-eyed people. Then, one day, I really took a look around, and almost everybody had two eyes. It hadn't happened! People still had their eyes. What a relief."

I listened carefully, but I kept watching him. He, as I, talks with his hands, even while eating. In one hand was a fork. Should he get too excited while talking, well, who knows, God forbid, where that fork could go?

It could take out a . . . Well, you know what I mean.

The Messiah Comes Tomorrow

The aunt was already now seventy-nine, and her husband was seventy-one, though he looked and acted older than his years because of the stroke he had suffered some time ago.

They had no children, the aunt and uncle. A couple of brothers here, a couple of sisters there. Not many left from that boatload out of Mother Russia, and what few were left were spread out all over Mother America.

Nobody ever visited them. This is not the America they came to, the one where, by force or design, the families clustered together in the same neighborhood. No, this is modern America. Mobile America. If, by some accident, a family is found together, it's given a fancy, shmancy name by the sociologists—the extended family.

So the two of them lived alone in a small apartment on the rear of the fourth floor in one of those look-alike buildings on Commonwealth Avenue. You know it? Where Brookline and Brighton and Newton kind of fall together.

The last shtetls in Boston. There is one now south of Dorchester in Hyde Park and parts of West Roxbury, where the Ward 14 immigrants were resettled. Pogroms have been replaced by blockbusting. There is another settlement across the city to the northwest in Brighton, where there survives yet even a Jewish political body of sorts with its own petitioner to the General Court.

Out in the northwest pale of settlement, life can be reasonable, what with rent control, the temples, the delicatessens, the small stores. Reasonable. But not filled with the joy and respect the talmudists say are the rights of old age.

Food is expensive. That's news? It was expensive before the big hoo-haa now. The four-block walk to the deli was getting longer for the aunt, and her husband could only shuffle with the help of a cane. A *shandeh un a charpeh*. A shame and a disgrace. That a woman once so active and a man with such a finely honed mind, an accountant, mind you, the only person who ever took the nephew to a *concert,* a real concert with an orchestra in a museum or someplace, that such people should be cooped up on the fourth floor, to the rear. A very long walk, when the elevator sticks.

So, the aunt was excited when she called the nephew. Their messiah had arrived. They had been accepted into Ulin House. Ulin House. A blessing on your house, Ulin House, *mazel-tov, mazel-tov.* It sits there, modern, brick, air-conditioned, on Wallingford Road, not far from where they lived. A promised land for those who never see Jerusalem. A place for older people to sit, to sing, to eat, to live, to entertain, to *kibbitz.*

There are two moods evident when you visit Ulin House. The mood of those who already live there, buoyant, secure, at last . . . something. And the mood of those who wait uncomfortably in the folding chairs of the dining room, wait for the volunteers to beckon them to a table, wait for the questions, for the decision on whether they enter the promised land this year, maybe next year, maybe never.

The aunt was excited, but nervous. She and her husband would be accepted as tenants at Ulin House. But they needed a guarantor. She pronounced it wrong. It's not enough they knew Russian, Yiddish, Hebrew and then had to learn English ("How can knife have a k in it? Why?"), but now, in their old age, they have to learn law.

Of course, he would be the guarantor, the nephew said. Don't worry, the aunt said, it doesn't obligate you to anything. Don't worry, the nephew said, he wasn't worried, so why should she worry? Nobody should worry. It was a typical Jewish-American conversation. The word *worry* was used at least sixteen times.

Twice, she read the nephew a letter about where he had to meet them and when. He would be there, he said, don't worry.

"Do you know something?" she said. "I understand they have at Ulin House refrigerators you don't have to defrost." At age seventy-nine, this is not too much to ask. Wonderful, said the nephew, who by the time he was thirty owned one of those. When he put down the receiver, he did two things. He cried just a little bit, and he began apologizing to God for all the kvetching he does.

So, everything was arranged. Two months before she could even move in, the aunt was already packing boxes. In that August heat, she began packing. They didn't have that much, but whatever they had, she would make sure it would be ready. The elderly are very careful people. At seventy-nine, you got to be ready.

The aunt took a stroke.

It happened about a week before she was going to sign the lease. The excitement, maybe? High blood pressure? Maybe in every elderly Jew, there is a *dybbuk,* a Cossack of the soul whose job it is to do whatever he can to keep you out of Jerusalem. Next year in Jerusalem, the Jews chant. Not if I can help it, says the *dybbuk.*

They took her to St. Elizabeth's, and for almost three days, her husband moved about alone, shuffled really, in that hot apartment. Life was confused. Nothing was right. It was difficult getting the laundry into the laundry bag. The beds were unmade. Papers were not where they belonged. The nephew came, huffing and puffing up the eight sets of stairs, afraid to take the elevator that might not work in such humidity.

In the uncle's eyes was fear. "What should we do? They won't let us move in, if somebody is sick."

At Ulin House, there was understanding. There was compassion. There was pity. And there are regulations.

The regulations say the tenant must be able to care for himself.

Next year in Jerusalem. When she's *better?* But Ulin House knew, and the nephew knew she would never be healthy enough to move in there. At the Ulin Houses of America, they deal daily with the disappointments of growing old in America.

They took her from St. Elizabeth's and put her in a nursing home, also in the neighborhood. He too moved in. At least there, he would eat regularly. You do not have to be told what it is like in a nursing home. Even a clean one, even one where the nurses kiss the patients, where the administrator takes time and talks with them. In the nursing homes, the tenants—the Jews, the Irish, the Italians, the blacks—they all begin to look alike to the visitor.

But even there, there is hope. Nu? There is yet some spark of hope, no? An aged Chinese lady who speaks Mandarin sits all day with her Armenian friend, who speaks only Armenian, and they talk, together. Ridiculous? Maybe. They too must fight the *dybbuks.*

One morning, the uncle did not respond to a nurse. Not the aunt—she was getting progressively worse. The uncle. He just sat in a chair, his mouth open. A stroke. When the nephew had seen him a few days before, the uncle had complained, "She can't tell me what's in her heart, and I can't tell her what's in mine." But he could at least sit there by the bed and hold her hand. Thirty-four years of marriage, and they held hands. Now, that too was rendered inoperative. This can no longer be allowed, said the Cossack.

They took him to St. Elizabeth's.

Then, on a Friday night, on *shabbes,* the doctor was called to the aunt's bedside. An aneurism in the aorta or something. Such words they have to learn. The heart gave out.

On Saturday, the devout Jews of the shtetl in Brighton

chanted in their synagogues. The New Year was coming. It was a time to remember the dead and pray for the happiness of the living, God should be good. That day, the nephew grew up a little bit. He shopped for caskets, he read through papers that dealt with memorial lots and bronze markers. Cancelled checks. Bills. Letters, old letters to the aunt and uncle about the rising price of bronze and how the cost must be passed off to the consumer.

It is difficult even to die in America. There are papers and forms and agencies to check with. And it is expensive. It costs the old-timers dearly to live. It costs them to die.

It was a short service on Sunday. The cantor spoke well and briefly of Rose Novick, a good and gracious woman. Ohmain. Amen. That afternoon, the nephew told the uncle, who lay there with a tube in his nose, about the funeral.

His options? To pass away. To go back to the nursing home? Whose hand would he now hold there? To try Ulin House again? No, there, they do not take the ill. Maybe, if he was lucky, someday, maybe, a room in the Hebrew Rehabilitation Center. "There's a long waiting list," the family was told. We know. We know. There are only so many trains out of Berlin, only so many planes out of Lisbon, only so many ships to America or Palestine. Only so many. And the lines are so long. So what else is new?

Jacob Novick tried to talk, but he could not. He tried to write a note, but it was hard for him to form the letters. He tried to cry. This, he could do.

Earlier that day, the nephew had watched on television a Jewish author talking to one of the few Jews left in Rumania, a bearded old *shochet,* the ritual slaughterer. The old man, himself the son of a butcher, had lost his family—his wife, children, parents, sister—to the Nazis. He survived. The Grand Rabbi of Rumania told him to go back to the few Jews in his province, not to Israel, but to Rumania, for without him, they would be like a flock without a shepherd. So, he went and stayed, performing his rituals for a rapidly dwindling population.

"*Shochet,*" the author asked the old man, "if you could have one wish from God, what would you wish for?"

"That the Messiah should come," he said.

"Would tomorrow be soon enough?" the author asked.

"Yesterday would have been too late already," the old man said.

A Stroll through the Old Neighborhood

She has come back to the old neighborhood, and it is still uncertain how she will leave it.

She is in a nursing home three streets from where they used to live in a small, second-floor apartment of a brown, wooden, two-story house.

"Do you remember," she asked the son late one Sunday afternoon, "how the waves used to crash over the roofs?"

Yes, Ma, he remembered.

He remembers a lot of things when he wanders through the old neighborhood.

Down the street from the back of the nursing home is the old red-brick elementary school. His father stayed out of work, and both parents took him to his first day of school on September something, 1943. In the school's asphalt yard, the kids played "Red Rover" and "Relievo" and fought one another over issues of religion and turf.

Where the nursing home is, a hotel used to be. Once, the community was full of hotels and rooms for rent in the summer. The town was even on postcards, one of which he stole one day after school from Max Sherman's drugstore right on the corner of the street where the nursing home now is.

He brought it home and gave it to his mother for a present. She took him back to the scene of the crime, and while she and Max tried hard not to laugh, he made his confession and promised never to stray again into the world of crime.

The hotel was a place that had seen more glorious days. "They had bar mitzvah receptions there," she told him the other day. "Women would dress in gowns to go there."

He had missed that era. He began hanging around the joint as a teenager, first because he thought his crowd ought to "take" the summer boys and, then, because he ' figured out that was dumb, and it seemed a lot more fun to hang around with the summer boys.

The summer boys came out of Roxbury, Dorchester, Mattapan, Brookline, Somerville, and such places. They swore that, back in their neighborhoods, there were girls who would do you know what, girls so tough that they would ambush the guys on the annual schoolboy parade and tear their epaulets off their uniforms. They brought stories of Roxbury Memorial and Dot High, of the Lewie in Mattapan and of the grand contests between English and Latin, both on and off the football field.

The winter boys and summer boys would play box ball on the hard mud at low tide and punch ball on the asphalt yard of the elementary school. On Sundays, they'd have enough guys to field two teams and play a double header of baseball on the town's one lousy ballfield. They would look for girls, and some of them would admit quietly that the only thing they really ever hoped to find was not so much a girl who would do you-know-what, but a girl who would at least talk to them. Some of them kept fighting, and some carried knives and wore sharpened garrison belts just in case.

And on rainy days, when the waters of the Atlantic began to roil, the boys would either hang around the hotel, shelter in a storm, or head back to his apartment, where they'd open the refrigerator and grab food and soft drinks, and kid around and make his parents smile and laugh a little. That would make for a nice break at home, which like the homes of a lot of guys back then, was not as happy as it should have been.

The home is different now, much nicer looking. Whoever has moved in has added to it, refurbished it.

Max Sherman is gone. The drugstore has been transformed into a small restaurant and coffee shop.

They're turning the school into condos.

The hotel deteriorated over the years: the story was

that local officials had condemned it, floor by floor, until there was nothing left to condemn. Now it's a nursing home, and the kid who used to hang around there for laughs now, as a man, goes there to bite his lip and wipe his eyes, to sit with his dad who's been feeling weak and down, to hold his mother's hand and struggle for the right things to say to the woman who took him to school down the street a long time ago.

"There were waves at the beach today, Ma."

"A storm is coming," she said.

Comforting New Generations

In the linen closet on the second floor of a house in Euless, Texas, is an afghan, a comforter knitted in designs of purple, red, and pink.

Esther did that a long time ago, back here in these parts, far from Texas. Esther knew Roxbury, Dorchester, Mattapan, Brookline. She knew Winthrop, Revere, Chelsea, and Malden. She didn't know from Texas. She was the ideal Greater Bostonian; this is where she grew up, this is where she died.

My mother's afghans were, like Joseph's coat, of many colors. The material was thick, as befits the very name "comforter." She worked hard on them, but she found it relaxing, and she gave them to the welcoming hands of family and friends.

"When I die," she used to joke, "they'll say, 'Esther? Esther? Oh, yeah, she made afghans.'"

When she died eight years ago, it turns out, people said and thought more than that. There are still those in the community who remember her as the one they went to see for some sympathy and for commonsense solutions to whatever ailed them.

Ironically, she could not address her own demons that plagued her for decades and made her unhappy and depressed, but she seemed able to console others.

In a gift too many cannot receive, she was given the chance to witness her two grandchildren become young adults. And now, in their adult homes in Texas and California, far away from Esther's small world, the afghans remain to comfort new generations.

She and her husband Max had never heard of Euless, a town down the road from Dallas. He was a traveling man, a salesman, and he had been to St. Louis by train and to New York and North Carolina and Maryland by car. He worked all six New England states every season of the year. But he had never been to Texas or California. Such adventures would be left to the next generation or two.

To Esther, this place called Euless would be a foreign land. There are no old apartment buildings all in a row, no tenements, no three-deckers, no fire escapes, no laundry flapping in the breeze, no small corner stores. Hell, no corners.

This is the land of malls and sprawl. Texas. Big country. Big plans. Big dreams. Big money. Euless is near Irving, the city where the Cowboys play football in a domed stadium with a hole in its roof, "So Gawd can look down at His team," as they say here.

This is a strange country for the children of Minsk, for people who grew up in crowded apartments and played jump rope or stickball in streets of traffic and went to old brick schools with asphalt playgrounds.

Euless is a place that knows whites, blacks, Latinos and Asians, but it stops there. The folks in these parts don't use the hyphens familiar to Esther's home turf. There seem to be no Italian Americans, Polish Americans, Irish Americans, Jewish Americans, Greek Americans.

They're here, of course, but they've all been blended into a great Caucasian morass. Most of the whites here are like the malls they go to for their food, clothing, and entertainment: They pretty much look alike.

Even if Esther were alive and reasonably healthy, she would not have visited this place. The spring, summer, and fall? Too hot. The winter? Who goes outside in the winter? Too many bugs. *Feh!* And they have snakes there, no?

But she loved the granddaughter, now in California, another strange place. And she loved the grandson, who came to Euless to make a family and a career, and she would have loved his wife and their daughter.

When her grandson left for Texas a few years ago, he

packed his Jeep with what he needed, including the afghan. He took it through states Esther never would have visited. He was on the road for three days, which would have impressed Max and frightened Esther.

Just as traditions and bittersweet memories are passed on from one generation to another, so too are objects, lovingly made and given with affection.

It may be that someday, ten years from now, when the grandson's daughter goes off to college, she might just take that afghan with her, as Esther's grandchildren did when they left to make their own lives.

Right now, at eight-and-a-half, she may not have the patience to listen to stories of great-grandparents she never knew. But someday, I, Esther's son, will take her aside and talk to her of people who came from other lands and of their offspring who grew up and died in and around Boston, and I'll take out the afghan just as a teller of folktales might hold up some object to illustrate a story.

Maybe she will finger it and somehow feel not only the strength of fibers, but also the bonds of history. In America, in strange and wondrous places far from where we start out, perhaps in such ways family and tradition manage to endure.

Memories of Max

The middle-aged man stands on the balcony of the New England Baptist Hospital and looks out over Mission Hill, Roxbury, Jamaica Plain, and beyond. From that vantage point, the scene resembles as much country as it does city, as if it were Northampton or Holyoke.

This is the back side of Boston, not the view the kids applying to colleges get in the brochures. Max, his old man, knew both sides—back and front. Max had worked for Filene's, and in the garment district, and in bars. He had lived at times in Roxbury and Dorchester, had hung around on Blue Hill Avenue with guys named Soapy and Spongy. He had shot pool at the corner of Morton and Blue Hill. He had played the numbers and waited for the runners with the good or bad news.

One year, he pitched for an elementary school in Roxbury—pitched southpaw, though he did pretty much everything else right-handed. Had a good season, he would say, but there were no pictures of him there or almost anywhere else. The family moved too often and didn't leave much history.

Max's parents didn't get along. There wasn't much love in the family. Even now, he still looks for the love he never had as a kid. When you grow up with so little, you sometimes cannot give of yourself. So, at times, he was loving and funny, and, at times, angry at the world, and self-centered.

Living is a tricky business. But dying is harder. That's what Max is doing a few feet down the hall from the balcony. He's fighting to live a little longer, but the heart is bad, and some of the other organs are not so good. And the medicine takes its toll on body, mind, and emotions.

The middle-aged son sits on a wooden bench on the balcony and stares hard at the old streets as if by so doing he could divine beyond what he already knows about what it was that helped mold his father. The message will not come. Too many offspring of immigrants squelched their emotions. History died as natural feelings were suffocated.

Max once was six feet tall, broad shouldered, and handsome as any movie actor. He was a strong man, a good boxer, a defender of his faith, a comic, and self-taught piano player in the Fats Waller school. It has been pitiful to see him shrinking, to see the clothes hanging on a fragile frame. He had been a clothing salesman most of his life and even now, in the hospital, can point to a doctor and guess his suit size.

He sold men's suits in Filene's for seventeen years, so you had to look sharp. Unlike his son, the *shlumpeh,* he took pride in dress. Now his clothes are old, wrinkled, and soiled. To go to the hospital, he packs them in a battered suitcase. When he was on the road for three decades, he carried a suitcase, a briefcase, a swatchbook, and sample bags with the pride of a "traveling man."

Those were the days before computers and big showrooms, the days when you bought a big car on payments, took your weekly money from a drawing account, worked for a pittance of a salary, prayed for good commissions, drove on icy roads, waited forever for small store owners to give you the time of day, crossed your fingers that the manufacturer wouldn't fold and screw you out of a few bucks, and drank and smoked too much "with the boys" in old downtown hotels.

Max makes it to eighty-two in the hospital. He eats some cake his daughter-in-law has baked. But he's weak. As the days drag on, he becomes confused. The son at times has to feed his father, as the father once fed the son when the son was but a baby.

Max hangs on for a while and then dies one cold night in the company of his other family—the doctors and nurses who had given him such extraordinary love and care.

Maybe the best epithet is what Arthur Miller wrote of Willy Loman in "Death of a Salesman": "Willy was a salesman. And for a salesman, there is no rock bottom to the life. He don't put a bolt to a nut, he don't tell you the law or give you medicine. He's a man way out there in the blue, riding on a smile and a shoeshine. And when they start not smiling back—that's an earthquake. And then you get yourself a couple of spots on your hat, and you're finished. Nobody dast blame this man. A salesman is got to dream, boy. It comes with the territory."

A House and Its Memories

In bits and pieces, two lives slowly disappear. What was home to my parents since 1957 is now just a piece of real estate, as bit by bit, piece by piece, I remove the physical evidence of two first-generation Americans who lived for eight decades.

This was the first and only home Esther and Max ever owned. She was fifty and he was forty-nine when they bought it, a single-family, five-room house in the center of town, an easy walk to shopping for a woman who never drove.

It was not as happy a home as it should have been, but it was theirs and was filled with what they thought was valuable, a term misused if one defines it only by money.

Now my wife and I clean it out. We practice a sort of triage. Some things are to be inherited; others to be given away; still others to be thrown into green plastic bags and left for the trash collectors.

My family will keep Esther's knitted afghans, the products of long and loving labor. "When I die," she used to joke, "will they remember me for anything? They'll say, 'She made nice afghans.'" She would be pleased to see grandson and granddaughter wrapped up to the neck in those afghans.

I collect Max's shirt studs and tie clips. Max had been a classy dresser. If proof be required, it is found in a drawer. There is a picture of Max as a young salesman at Filene's. A full head of black hair parted in the middle, penetrating hazel eyes, a classy suit, and a colorful red pinstriped shirt.

What is to be kept? What is to be given away? What is to be thrown out? I wonder who made me God all of a sudden. I never wanted the power to dispose of the remains of the lives of others. I want to keep everything, all the pots and pans, all the dishes and cutlery, all the towels and furniture polish. My wife smiles. She has been through this before; she played God for her own parents.

You have to be tough. You have to keep telling yourself that when you throw out a skillet that even the poor could not use, you are not throwing out the memories of your parents or your own past. Memories are more than a collection of items.

The house looks a lot better than it has in many years. A new heating unit is humming away in the basement. Rugs have been pulled up. Floors, doors, and cabinets have been varnished. Ceilings and walls are freshly painted.

The house is becoming aseptic, devoid of the presence of its former occupants and visitors. It becomes a place to be marketed to someone else. New lives will begin here, as the inevitable process of regeneration goes on thirty-four years after the only people known to this house have left it. It must be that way. So goes the rebirth of neighborhoods.

When I drive down another street, the one where I grew up, I always look at the family's old apartment, the one we left thirty-four years ago. I don't know the names of the occupants or most of their neighbors. Only one person, I believe, is left from the 1940s and '50s.

And thirty-four years from now, who in my parents' last neighborhood will know or care that the couple who lived in this five-room house bridged the history of a nation from its first decade to, in the case of my father, its last? From a deadly influenza epidemic to cures for cancer. From trenches in France to trenches in Kuwait. From horses and wagons to space travel. From two-cent newspapers to cable television. From parents who spoke in the tongues of Europe to cookie-cutter American kids who all talk, like, you know, the same.

In truth, the world of Max and Esther had begun disappearing long before their demise. Gone were the dance halls, social clubs, and speakeasies of their youth. Few remained of the department stores and clothing outlets. Long gone was the twenty-five-cent lunch at Kresge's or the trilby (egg and onion sandwich) at Hayes-Bickford. Buildings, streets, whole neighborhoods had changed or even disappeared. Familiar landmarks went the way of old friends and relatives.

Once a local television crew came to interview them about the radio scare that Orson Welles had created in 1938 with his realistic production of "The War of the Worlds," and, often, I would sit and listen to the talk of old days. With its pictures, pots and pans, and paraphernalia from the early 1900s through the 1960s, the house became testimony to history. In history, there is refuge for the aging, an ally in a nation that pays scant attention to either the old or its own history.

Now, I finally cancel the phone service. I had delayed doing so by rationalizing that I might need to use the phone. I rarely did. It became an unnecessary expense. There is something definitive about canceling phone service, about knowing that for the first time in thirty-four years you cannot call that number.

In time, when the final decisions are made on possessions, new people will come to rent or buy the house. I hope they will flourish. I hope also that maybe they will wonder, once in a great while, about the people who lived here before them—people who, for all their faults and virtues, were part of a family and a small part of what America once was.

Thanks, but It's Too Late

To: Phillip Riese
    Executive Vice President
    AMERICAN EXPRESS

Dear Sir:

This is in regard to your invitation to Maxwell Lupo to apply for the American Express Card.

As the person who handles Max's vast financial holdings, I wish to thank you so much not only for the invitation but also for the manner in which it was delivered.

As you wrote, membership "is accorded only to those who have achieved a certain measure of financial success."

I couldn't agree more. My father Max also would agree, but he faces a niggling little detail that prevents him from taking you up on your kind offer. Perhaps I can explain by referring to the invitation card accompanying your letter. "American Express Card membership," it said. "Perfectly suited to the way you live."

There is no tactful way to put this, but I shall try. Uh, the way Max lives is that he doesn't. He has not been living at all since January of 1991, when he died. This state of affairs raises serious questions about the phrase, "perfectly suited."

Even before he died he was not exactly living in a style to which most of your cardholders may be accustomed. The man was on Social Security. He showed up at restaurants for the early-bird specials. He got discounts on the T. He had a black-and-white television set that defied reception on at least one VHF and two UHF channels.

No matter how many hours he spent near the phone, neither Jackie, nor Liz, nor any of that fast-moving crowd ever called. A jet-setter he wasn't. A big day out was driving to Chelsea for a hot corned beef on a bulkie, and then only if the dentures were working right. He used to get angry when the guy who mowed his lawn asked for money.

The big question is this: Where were you guys when it counted? Where were you in the early part of the century when the repo men used to show up at Max's mother's place and take back the piano? Where were you later on when Max was out of work?

I am upset that some of Max's big financial opportunities have come a bit late. It was almost a year after he died that Reader's Digest informed him that he had a shot at the $5 million prize in the company's sweepstakes. "A strict computer selection process" managed to place Max close to that jackpot that he and his friends used to dream about in the old days.

Max, by the way, worked hard and finally made a good living, but he and guys like him never stopped dreaming about what you might call a milestone.

In your letter you noted, "The road to financial success has many milestones marking how far you've come."

Max had a few of those. There was the time, for example, when he was relaxing at a joint three blocks from our apartment and decided to try his luck at the slot machine. Just before he plunked in his quarter, the resident dog whizzed on the base of said machine.

Max played the quarter anyway and was rewarded with a large pile of change. For the next two weeks the gentlemen frequenting this establishment tried in vain to convince the doggie to relieve himself on the machine.

They called this financial planning. I would call this a milestone. But to Max and others like him, getting a credit card was not such a milestone, no disrespect intended, sir. No, they thought making it financially was being able to pay the bills as they came in and have a little something left over for themselves and their kids.

But you and I know, of course, that such thinking is old-fashioned, that credit is king, that buying on credit is a lot easier and, well, costlier than playing the slots, and that's why this nation is in the fine shape it's in today.

We are careful, of course, as to who gets credit. But your letter proves that buying on credit is the right of almost every living American—and then some.

On Christmas Eve, a Toast to Two Who Cared

Tonight is for Helen and Hugh.

Christmas was their holiday, which they wrapped like a cloak around an unshaven soldier who had traveled all night and day to see their daughter, with whom he was, and is, in love.

Two cultures met that night and forged a bond that even death could not break. Theirs was English and Irish Catholic and German Lutheran—old wines in an American bottle—with a family bible inscribed with the names of babes born in the early 1800s and stories of great-uncles and cousins who fought on both sides of the Mason-Dixon line. His was Romanian and Russian Jewish, short-timers yet in the refuge of America, still wise guys not far from bouncing on the street corners of urban America. Norman Rockwell meets Henny Youngman.

They were stand-up people who felt at home and believed deeply in America, one worth fighting for to preserve its promise for all citizens. They had worked their way through law school during the Depression.

Hugh later left the lucrative private sector to devote his professional life to the unappreciated art of judging when to parole felons. Helen jumped into politics and took on the pols and the bureaucrats on behalf of the helpless. Hugh enlisted in World War II, even though he was old enough to have avoided it. They were believers.

They taught their daughter that life was not an onerous burden to be feared, but a challenge that one should meet as a happy warrior. She has done so. Her husband is still learning.

Helen and Hugh cared about those who did not live on their tree-lined street, those who had suffered—the alcoholics, the elderly, the infirm, the poor. They knew nothing changed overnight, but that the fight to help others had to be fought nevertheless. It could be fought with a sense of irony, with a laugh, with an impish grin at the foibles of humankind, with love and compassion. They were New Dealers, but not ideologues. They were fighters, but not kamikaze crusaders. In memory of them, the son-in-law thinks this Christmas Eve of the others.

He wonders about the little black kid in the village of Woodridge, New York. Almost thirty years ago, the mother was whacking the kid pretty hard, and being young and knowing little caution, the reporter jumped into the crowd and stuck a fake pistol in the mother's face. The kid grabbed the young man and hugged him and looked up with fear in his eyes. One of the men in the crowd said everything would be cool.

That kid would be about thirty now, if he lived, if he survived the poverty of spirit and soul that afflicted him and his neighbors. To this day, the man remembers what the mother said, as much in resignation as in challenge. "Shoot me!" she yelled. "I don't care."

He wonders about the white women who worked Baltimore's version of the Combat Zone twenty-two years ago. They were in their twenties, most of them, some of them fresh from the mountains of Kentucky and West Virginia. They were B-girls, paid to hustle customers for drinks, maybe to peddle some flesh. They were good kids, most of them. It was better to be their friend than to be their customer. They liked having guys, even slob reporters from City Hall, to talk to, knowing nothing was expected. He wonders how they survived—if they survived—the mean streets.

He wonders now about today's people, here in Massachusetts. The other day, Debbie Weinstein, director of the Massachusetts Human Services Coalition, gave Governor Dukakis a letter at a closed-door meeting. It read, in part:

"One-quarter of the babies born this year will be on welfare at some point by their second birthday. Putting them at risk of inadequate nutrition and housing during their crucial developmental years exacts a cost we will all pay in countless ways.

"In the short term, incomes too low to make ends meet lead to homelessness, impaired health, and interrupted education. In the longer term, we pay in lost resources for our labor force and in additional needs for various forms of institutional care."

He wonders if too many of us have become so inured to poverty, violence, and desperation that we have given up any pretense of fighting it. For too long, we have not experienced the spirit of taking on the odds that characterized the Washington of FDR, Truman, and Kennedy; the Washington that Helen and Hugh knew and believed in.

They would have kept caring, and, if health allowed, kept fighting. When he raises that glass to them tonight, it is not only to their memory but also to the promise to stay the course and try to manage to have a few laughs along the way.

As the Youngmans might have said to the Rockwells, "*L'chaim,* old friends."

The Continuity of Family

They drove through Boston's South End, and though the man was unabashedly choking up, he managed to sputter out something about the continuity of family.

He told his wife that his father was born on the New York Streets, a South End neighborhood that later became a melting pot of all kinds of Americans and was obliterated by urban renewal. Anyway, his father was born in a tenement in 1908, and now, here were the son and his wife crossing the old turf to his own son's graduation at Northeastern.

For the grandfather, the son of Romanian and Russian immigrants, poverty was a staple of childhood, and college was nothing more than a dream. Now the grandson was about to get a master of science degree in criminal justice. For each generation there has been a rule, usually unspoken: learn from the book and learn from the street. Continuity.

Now the couple sits in the Matthews Arena, and they look about them. Look, look at the audience and at the graduates. Look at the faces, the white ethnic of every stripe, the black of Africa and the West Indies, the Asian and the Latino.

Eat your heart out, Europe. You never did get it. You starved and evicted your Irish, turned your back on your Italians and Poles and Slavs, persecuted your Jews. You even now reject the Arabs and Asians and Africans who come to you for succor.

Eat your heart out, Europe. You still don't get it. And you are the poorer for it, and America is the richer for it. Look at the graduates marching in and believe it.

Up in the galleries, the families begin yelling and whistling. The elements of this peculiarly North American mix cluster at the arena's rail and are now photographers edging for position as if they were at a political convention.

Yes, good. Laugh, shout, whistle and, yes, cry too. They celebrate their kin and their kind, their blood and their diversity.

Maya Angelou, the commencement speaker, understands. She, black, out of Stamps, Arkansas, the once mute child become renaissance person—author, poet, actress, journalist, orator. She begins not with oration but with song. "Look where you've all come from," she chants repeatedly and then speaks to the graduates of the past, of the continuum. She knows that, at their age, maybe they do not spend much time thinking of what preceded them, of what helped make them look and behave the way they do, of what transpired to put them in those academic robes.

She wants to remind them of all this, she says, but also to talk of where they are going and "where you are taking us." So she begins describing what the middle-aged guy had begun thinking about on his way through the South End.

The poet-orator talks of Irish escaping the potato blight, of Jews escaping pogroms, of Chinese brought here to do backbreaking labor and never allowed to bring their wives, of Africans chained to the decks and lying in their own vomit.

"They did for each of you already without ever knowing what your faces would look like," she says. "They did for you. It is important to know that, to stop and see who came before you."

She tells them she carries with her everywhere the people of her little Arkansas town. "I never denied them. You must not deny anybody who helps you along the way."

There is a legacy at stake this evening. A baton is passed from one generation to the next, to the next and the next.

We are, all of us, not individuals only, as we have been led to believe lately. We are a community and need one another.

"Not enough of us," Angelou says modestly, "have told you how desperately we need you."

A man was born in 1908. The tenement in which he was born was razed. The street was wiped off the map. The man lived eighty-two years. At a memorial service for his wife, the old man looked at his grandchildren and choked up and said, "The legacy." The son nodded, perhaps even a bit impatient at the sentiment, yet understanding it in his gut.

You can destroy a tenement and wipe out a street. You can take one's ancestors to their final rewards. But you do not lightly break the continuum. You must not deny the dreams.

CHAPTER TWO

Comfortable? It's a Living

Jews were not always CEOs, corporate lawyers, bigtime real estate developers, and chiefs of surgery.

Of course, some were, and the rest of us were very happy for them, God bless them and let them go in peace.

In my youth, there were plenty of Jews who worked with their hands and used their wits, as in street smarts. They were the working stiffs.

On my street, one guy, Hy, was a milkman. Another, Carl, was a butcher. My Uncle Saul Rosenberg was a butcher. My best pal's dad worked all night in a deli as a sandwich maker. There were glaziers, carpenters, cabbies, pants pressers, cops, and crooks.

They wanted more for their kids, so they pushed us to go to college. So? We went. And what happens when you go to college? You tend to move someplace else, someplace where your parents are not. Then, your old community begins to die along with the parents, the butchers, milkmen, glaziers, pressers, wiseguys. It is a self-fulfilling prophecy.

To understand ourselves and where we came from, it is important to know how many of us made a living—indeed, how some of us still do.

Not always with the suit and the nice watch and the shiny shoes.

Where a Sigh Can Speak Volumes

Some guys get their fix from neighborhood drug dealers; some, from the local saloon or package store. Me? I go to Harvard Street in Brookline, where you get two fixes for the price of one—the kind of food that enabled you to develop a childhood immunization to acidity, and the kind of culture that reminds you that whatever you finally became, a big shot you're not.

As Passover approaches, I am standing in line with a basket of food in The Butcherie. Moses had less of a wait before the Red Sea opened.

In front of me are two elderly women who have driven in from Malden. One walks with an aluminum walker. The other is the designated driver and choreographer of the shopping trip.

The driver is paying with cash. She needs another buck. She yells to her companion, "Do you have a dollar? They need another dollar."

The woman with the walker has her wallet, but she's not making any moves to get the buck.

The driver yells, "Give her a dollar. They need another dollar."

The woman with the walker yells back—understand that we are so close together that we resemble a Green Line car in rush hour—"I heard you the first time. You think I'm not listening? She (pointing to the cashier) is busy. I don't want to interrupt. I heard you."

The cashier, a Russian Jew, is indeed trying to explain something to the bagger. The bagger is a thin, middle-aged guy with a visored cap, the visor of which is pointed straight up. He seems not to understand the various languages being directed at him—English, Russian, Yiddish. But he smiles and is working hard. God bless America.

The woman with the walker is trying to tell him to

double-bag something. She uses a Yiddish word. From behind the bagger comes another voice—another country heard from—another guy with another visored cap who says, "He doesn't understand. He's Portuguese."

I perk up at that. I asked the cashier, "Is he a Sephardic Jew?"

The Russian cashier smiles and wants to know what I am talking about. I ask again.

"I don't know," she says, "we can't communicate."

What she means is that they do not communicate in depth. But communicate, they do. We may be second-generation Americans, or Russian immigrants, or Israeli visitors. We may be Sephardic Jews from Spain, Portugal, or North Africa or Ashkenazi Jews from Europe or Russia. We may be Reform, Conservative, Orthodox, or agnostic Jews. But we communicate, if not with words, then, at least with our hands, eyes or grunts.

So, then, the reader must understand what The Butcherie is. It is, of course, a store filled with food. The aisles are narrow. So, it is also a place filled with people who regard food as the reason we left Egypt in the first place.

You do forty years in the desert with nothing to eat but matzoh, you end up cranky and with cramps. A land of milk and honey is tantalizing. A land of potato latkes and stuffed cabbage is a place worth hanging around, even if the aisles are narrow.

Many of those maneuvering the shopping carts up and down those aisles are not doing so easily, given the lay of the land. Also, a fair number of them are no longer fleet of foot. On top of that, they push carts the way we all drive in this state.

But I do the reader an injustice, for I have not yet finished setting the scene. The store is more than a store. Like other stores up and down Harvard Street, this place is part of the last real urban *shtetl,* or Jewish village, in these parts. In this particular establishment, a variety of Jews buy goods from Russian Jews. You can hear Yiddish. And you can hear Russian. And you can hear versions of English that do not resemble the King's. Unless we are talking King David or King Solomon.

Now, the driver sees the people lined up behind her and her friend with the walker. She is stricken with guilt. If you think we are crazy with food, you should see us with guilt.

"I'm sorry to hold you up," she says. "We're both sick."

She says this with a sigh that comes from the depths of her being, a sigh of the ages, a sigh that cannot be described in words, but is familiar to every patron in the store. It is redolent of every sigh that every patron's grandmother ever heaved up into the ozone. It can mean anything from, "Napoleon's retreat from Moscow was no picnic," to, "Who is Jose Canseco, such a big shot, he has to go on strike?" It is an all-inclusive exclamation that manages to wrap up about 5,000 years of aggravation in one syllable.

"No problem," I say, for who, in this season of remembrance and charity, could deny a sigh such as that? And I even throw in a "Take your time." All this, despite the strain of a metal shopping basket that includes three containers of chicken soup, two containers of matzoh balls, one package of stuffed cabbage, one, of miniature potato latkes and one, of vegetable kugel.

On my right, a woman waits with her shopping cart, facing at a left angle to mine. She and I exchange knowing glances. The Jewish knowing glance is not as dramatic as the sigh, but is sufficiently explicit, what with a nod of the head to the left or right, concurrent with a raising of both eyebrows.

The woman with the walker has forked over a buck for her friend and is now paying for her own food by check. Paying by check takes longer than paying by cash. Now it is her turn to be stricken with guilt, and she turns to those behind her. Before she can sigh, I smile my best reassuring anti-guilt don't-worry-about-it smile.

In a situation like this, you have to be on your toes. You must be aware not only of shoppers who ram into you or your cart but also of the signals—the sighs, the nods, the grunts, the looks, the verbal asides made to no one in particular but meant to be heard nevertheless—and you must be ready to react.

A verbal aside such as, "I would love to look at the chicken," usually means, "You, *shmendrick,* you have to stand there all day in front of the chicken? You're a young man. You have your whole life to stand in front of chickens. I'm an old lady. God only knows how many years I have left to breathe, much less to stand yet."

Because I would know what such a comment really means, I must be ready and willing to move at a second's notice. I could, of course, stand there just for spite and refuse to let an oldtimer get to the pullets. If it were a younger person, I might do so. But to an older person? I might as well stab her in the heart.

The point, I suppose, dear reader, is this:

When you go shopping in such a place, you should not be in a hurry. After all, we are celebrating the exodus from Egypt, where we had lousy jobs at no wages. Here, we can afford food, so why complain about waiting for it? We are remembering those forty years in the desert. What's a few minutes in a cashier's line compared to forty years? The blink of an eye is what.

The two ladies struggle outside with their goods. It is my turn. I have one more act of charity to perform. I speak to the bagger in Spanish and apologize for not knowing Portuguese. He grabs my right hand and shakes it, and smiles and answers. All day long, he has been bagging without hearing a familiar voice. Now, he has heard something Iberian.

"You speak Portuguese?" the Russian cashier asks. But I walk out fast. Much as I like to spend time there, I cannot afford to give up my day job and become a bagger translator.

Then again, if the bottom falls out of the newspaper business . . .

Drucker, Murder, Inc., Hoodlum, Dies in Prison

Jack Drucker, a Hurleyville farmer who made his name in the ranks of Murder, Inc., died yesterday in his cell at Attica State Prison, where he was serving twenty-five years to life for second degree murder.

An autopsy showed Drucker, fifty-six, died of a coronary occlusion. The former syndicate strongarm man left a wife and two daughters.

Drucker was tried and convicted in 1944 in Sullivan County Court for the ice-pick murder of Walter Sage, coordinator of the syndicate's slot machine operation in the Catskills.

The trial was the first courtroom case for Benjamin Newberg as a district attorney and attracted wide attention.

Drucker, then thirty-nine, had been indicted on five counts of first degree murder. The co-defendants as named on the indictment were the stars of Murder, Inc., the syndicate's own enforcement squad which made murder a nationwide business.

Sullivan County was a playground for many of the criminal elite. For at least seven gentlemen, it became a cemetery. One of those seven was Walter Sage.

Sage was doing well in his Catskill niche until certain mob elements noted some deficiencies in the treasury. It was decided that the deficiencies warranted punishment. Sage had to go and go he did—right into Swan Lake in the summer of 1937.

When the body was found, it was noted that he had been stabbed thirty-two times with an ice pick, tied up, weighted down with a slot machine, and thrown into the lake.

A few years later, Irv (Gangy) Cohen was picked up in

Hollywood by Sullivan County law officials. Both Cohen and Drucker were implicated in the Sage murder.

Cohen was acquitted, but Drucker, defended by the brilliant criminal lawyer Hyman Barshay, was convicted in the trial before the late County Judge George L. Cooke. Barshay is now Kings County Judge.

Long before Drucker's trial, Murder, Inc. was breaking apart at the seams. The law was bearing down on the boys from Brownsville and Ocean Hill. First, the bit players began to talk, then, the stars.

One of the "talkers" at Drucker's trial was Albert (Allie) Tannenbaum, whose family was in the resort business at Rock Hill and Loch Sheldrake.

Tannenbaum had been named in two of the Drucker counts, one involving the murder of Irv Ashkenaz, a taxicab owner, and the other, the killing of Hy Yuran, a garment dealer.

Tannenbaum began talking in 1940 to Sullivan County District Attorney William Deckelman, now a State Supreme Court Judge. His testimony and that of "Pretty" Levine cinched the case against Drucker.

The jury returned a verdict of guilty to second degree murder. Judge Cooke sentenced Drucker to Clinton State Prison at Dannemora for twenty-five years to life.

Drucker had gone through the eighth grade. At the time he was sentenced, his mother was living, his father, dead. He had already been married. He gave his occupation as "farmer." It was on the Drucker farm that officials found the body of Charles (Chink) Sherman, another of the mob's victims.

Drucker appealed in 1945, but got nowhere. Two years later, Judge Cooke dismissed on Barshay's request the four other counts against Drucker.

By that time, Drucker had been in Sing Sing, Clinton, and Auburn Prisons. He was then sent to Attica, where he assumed the number 10969.

10969 has died, perhaps more peacefully than did many of his cohorts. When Murder, Inc. broke down, it took part of the syndicate with it, and some of the board members went all the way to the electric chair.

Used Clothing Store Brings "Block" Madison Ave. Pitch

Two gentlemen of wanderlust nature were standing in front of Henry Becker's secondhand clothing store on The Block and were admiring a pair of abominable blue checkered pants.

"World's Fair pants," read the sign, a piece of cardboard marked with black crayon. "Just arrived from Yenna Velt," a Yiddish expression, which, translated freely, refers to the other world.

"Where's Yenna Velt?" asked the first with a strong Kentucky accent.

"It's a small town outside of Chicago," answered his cosmopolitan friend.

"Oh yeah," said the first, "we passed through there."

That is the kind of conversation engendered by Mr. Becker's signs, advertising everything from a single shoe to a suit jacket of Al Capone vintage.

Mr. Becker buys, sells, and repairs secondhand clothing. For twenty-two years, from 8 A.M. to 6 P.M. six days a week, Mr. Becker has bought, sold and repaired second-hand clothing. When someone asks him if he ever gets tired of it all, he says, with a shrug, "Yeah, every day."

In the 600 block East Baltimore street he runs a shop with two sections, one for working and one for relaxing. The one for working is the larger section in front, complete with racks of cloths, old tables, a pants presser, a sewing machine, tape measures, a hook of belts, and outdated calendars with pictures of girls who are very much up to date.

"If they ever come back," Mr. Becker says, pointing to a rack filled with double-breasted, wide-lapel suits, "I'll be a millionaire."

The back section is smaller, it houses a refrigerator, a

supply of chopped herring and a place to eat and relax with people who drop by.

"Some of them are a little particular, though," he says of those who partake of free lunch offerings. "They don't like chopped herring."

Mr. Becker, a short, pleasant, balding man, contends between puffs of a cigar that his signs do not bring in so much business, but they give people a laugh.

"One day, I come in to open the store," he says, "and there it is, a perfectly good shoe. What am I gonna do with a shoe?"

What he did was to display it in his front window with a sign that displays all the come-on of a Madison Avenue plug: "Bring in the other shoe and get this one free."

"You'd be surprised. All kinds of people stop to read those signs," says Sam Votopsky, the barber next door. "High-class people, low-class people, boys, girls, women, men. They even come from across the street."

Mr. Becker pulled out a pair of wide, black seaman's boots from under a table and brushed off clouds of dust with a small broom. One of the boots had been cut off at the bottom.

The pair was offered as having belonged to "Captain Bligh—chewed off by a shark in Mutiny on the Bounty."

In the right-hand corner of the show window is a double-breasted, wide-striped, wide-lapel suit on a headless mannequin. "Worn by the Untouchables," says the sign. "We have them in all colors."

"If you want cuffs put on your pants fast," reads another, "$1."

"Half-fast . . . 98 cents."

"Some who come in here are panhandlers and smoke-hounds who'll sell anything for a drink," says the fifty-five-year-old former East Baltimore resident. "But to look at some of the people who come in, it can tear your heart out."

Burlesque Comedian Reminisces about Early Days—and the Changes

In the littered dressing room of a Baltimore burlesque house, Dick Bernie sat and chewed a piece of gum and smoked and talked about the slow death of an era.

He is a comedian, and because of that, he could look at the walls where the paint had fallen away in spots and say, "Gee, isn't that a nice design."

He talked about his stint with Earl Carroll's "Vanities" and George White's "Scandals" and a man named Al Jolson.

"I gotta show you somethin'," he said to a visitor. He pulled out from his wallet a picture, brown with age, showing a younger Bernie clowning to a smiling Jolson.

"To me, he was the greatest. He used to sing a song in Yiddish. I think it was 'The Tailor, the Rabbi and the Shoemaker.' I always used to ask him to sing that one for me. When I heard he died, I cried."

The sun was shining outside, but the only light in the room came from an electric bulb. No daylight crept through the one window, painted black.

The dressing table was cluttered with change, makeup, clothing, and the items that can gather in a man's pockets. An undershirt hung on a hook. In one corner, sitting in a hat, was an empty bottle. It did not belong to Dick Bernie.

"Show business isn't like people think, always drinking and going crazy. I don't bother with that. I had an experience with one partner after I got out of Earl Carroll's 'Vanities.' I told him we couldn't work together unless he stopped drinking, and he did.

"We were really flying. We were young and fresh. But somehow he got back on it. He's blind today."

The door to the dressing room was partly opened, and the one-two throb of the drummer boomed across the back stage. The trumpet screamed "Caravan."

55

Dick Bernie had done one skit. He was waiting to go on for a second. From noon until 11 P.M., he would do a total of eight. The pay is not great, it is said, but it's steady.

"The only time you get tired is from hanging around the theater from 12 to 5. They're not what they used to be. Years ago, you'd have a line of girls, a boy singer, two comics, and two straight men.

"They just don't have as many stagehands to handle the scenery. You just do your jokes with maybe a chair and a table."

He puffed on a filter-tipped cigarette. His face was serious, but soft and capable of being molded into a dozen different Greek tragicomic expressions.

"I think burlesque is the greatest school for comedians or any entertainers, but it's changed. There's no place today for anybody to come up, to learn timing. You've got to have timing, whether you're a comic or a straight man."

For almost forty of his fifty-six years, Dick Bernie has been a comic. When his name was Bernstein in New York City, he was a credit man in a cotton goods house.

"But I got a job in a road act. I was in show business six years without my family knowing it. Every time we went outta town, I told my folks I was checking accounts."

Dick Bernie has played it straight and has been the clown. He has danced and even fiddled. He has worked in television, movies, and on the stage, from opening nights on Broadway to Wednesday nights in Dayton.

"I think this is a great business. Take another man my age. He would look like my father. You keep yourself young by always joking and always clowning on and off stage."

He said he was heavier, and his well-combed, thick hair is partly gray, but he is not quitting.

"Once you get it into your blood, it's hard to quit. You can take the ham out of a pig, but you can't take it out of an actor."

Dick Bernie has understudied the likes of Benny and

Berle. "Always the bridesmaid and never the bride," he called himself. He has done better than perform for the afternoon crowd at a burlesque house, but the work is steady and it keeps a man busy.

"My wife was thirty-nine when she died last year," he said. "I've got to keep my mind occupied. It's not corny when they say the 'show must go on.' The audience doesn't realize how much heartbreak you can have inside of you.

"I went out once when she was very sick. I went out there with tears in my eyes, and I hadda make people laugh. It's like the clown, under a mask."

Dick Bernie had to stop talking. He had to go on. He waited in the wings while the straight man and the blonde began a routine. It was a dead audience.

There was a cue, and Dick Bernie, comedian, ran out on stage with a ridiculous hat and a checkered jacket. And the audience laughed.

A Bad Bet

Howard Levenson seems nervous. At times he smiles, but he is pacing back and forth in the corridor outside U.S. District Court Room No. 3 on the twelfth floor of the federal courthouse in Post Office Square, and he sporadically shushes his friends, Jimmy Katz and Richie Weinstein, because he worries that their voices will disrupt proceedings behind the swinging doors of justice.

Katz is one of those guys who has mastered the art of conversing with his lips almost clenched, but Weinstein has the mouth of a vaudevillian. Both techniques are common to those of us who grew up urban and Jewish.

Katz and Levenson, bookmakers, are waiting to negotiate sentencing on plea bargains. They have admitted to money laundering, which, in their case, meant taking checks from customers and cashing them in various joints, one of which was owned by Michael London, alleged banker to the bookies.

Weinstein says he's not a bookmaker, just a bettor. He and others also have been plea bargaining on the money laundering charge. Their turn comes later. Weinstein is there to be with his friends and get an idea of what may be in store for him.

Because the money laundering charge is more serious than a bookmaking charge, Katz and Levenson are looking at hard time. While Levenson paces and Weinstein does the color commentary, Katz wonders out loud what is happening in this country.

"The government is turning everyone into rats," he says. "It's not good for society. You're always lookin' behind you. It'll become like Russia."

What's really going on here is what remains unspoken later during the court proceedings. Burton (Chico) Krantz, who grew up with these guys in Dorchester and Mattapan, has become what wise guys call a rat, as in, one who rats on his pals.

That Krantz, a longtime big shot bookie, has been cooperating with the law for a couple of years now came as shocking news to his old associates. Now the feds are hoping that by hitting Katz, Levenson, and others with stiff sentences, they can "turn" them also. Into rats.

"I won't do that," Katz says. "I'm not built that way. Because a man is a man doesn't mean he should be penalized."

Levenson stops his pacing to come over and note, "The government is practicing extortion."

The government hopes that if it turns enough guys, it will be able to make a case against Whitey Bulger, Steve (The Rifleman) Flemmi, and Francis (Cadillac Frank) Salemme.

Later, in court, Assistant U.S. Attorney Brian Kelly says Katz and Levenson make extortion payments to organized crime.

U.S. District Judge Rya Zobel says, "That's not part of this case, so let's not talk about it."

It is, however, part of the federal strategy in going after big shots, which is why, Katz complains, "every other day, they call me. 'You wanna go with Chico?'" He laughs. "I say, 'Yeah, but I don't know where he is.'"

Chico is in hiding.

But Katz and Levenson have no place to go but into the courtroom, where Katz's attorney, Robert Sheketoff, argues, "This is not traditional money laundering where people are trying to launder dirty money into clean money."

Katz, he says, is a bookmaker and has been for some time. If charged with bookmaking, the sentence would be halved. "Instead, the government, being clever, turned him into a money launderer. He'd have preferred cash. Drug dealers and bookmakers should not be considered the same."

Customer convenience is the issue, Katz and Weinstein have explained. Bookmaking is a business, and if the customers want to pay in checks, what can you do but take them? Business is not what it used to be anyway, many bookies say. So why stay in it?

It's how they grew up. They played cards. They shot pool in Cutler's pool room on Blue Hill Avenue. That's what they know.

Katz gets four years. Levenson gets thirty months. Katz's wife and daughters are hugging him and crying, and all over America, spouse abusers and armed thugs do less time. Go make book on that craziness.

Sticking by the Union

A good Labor Day to you.

My father, Max, worked out of the garment district in Boston. I should say my late father, Max, and the late garment district, though remnants of that commercial neighborhood survive.

He worked for Henry Levine Tru-Proportioned Slacks, which meant that he traveled all over New England, opening accounts in store after store for those merchants smart enough to see a big boom coming in Bermuda shorts and pedal pushers for women.

Thanks to my father's hard work and my mother's ability to save money, I went to college, where my attempts to get dates with young women in Bermuda shorts fell somewhat short of my father's ability to peddle the stuff.

Max—like his twin brother, Leo, like his brother-in-law, Bobby Silverman, like most traveling salesmen—regarded himself as an independent sort of guy, what one might today call an entrepreneur. Salesmen, for the most part, belonged to associations, which gave them some benefits, but not to unions.

Salesmen had mixed feelings about unions. They didn't trust them, but they were jealous of the benefits and perks that union members managed to win over the years.

"My contract?" my father told me one day. "My contract was a handshake fourteen years ago. So if [his boss] wants to break my contract, what can I do? Give him an ultimatum? In a plant, everybody—the shippers, the packers—has protection, but the salesmen who feed the whole machine get nothing."

So, then, Dad, why not organize and join a union?

"Nah," he would say, raising his eyelids all-knowingly. Even in the 1950s, the heyday of American unions, a number of working stiffs, like my father, could not bring themselves to join the organized labor movement.

After all, there had been Lepke—Louis (Lepke) Buchalter—and his fellow wiseguys and leg breakers, Jewish and Italian mobsters, who had infiltrated the unions in the 1930s and whose influence was alleged to still be felt a quarter century later. Of course, the Mob had infiltrated management too, but that seemed to create less fear among salesmen.

Perhaps the "traveling man," as each called himself, was the ultimate optimistic American, who, then and now, believed that one can make it on one's own. There is some truth to it, of course, but it is largely a grand myth that grows increasingly irrelevant as businesses suck up businesses, as corporations become megacorporations and as progressive thinkers preach that management-union teamwork and workers' circles and such are the way of the future.

Some of my father's attitude toward unions may have stemmed from an incident involving his own father, Isaac, a Romanian Jewish immigrant, who took his family from Boston to Stoughton early this century to look for work.

One day, Isaac and other job seekers were taken to a mill. But outside the mill was a picket line of men, either union men protesting conditions and wages or just workers trying to organize a union. An Italian immigrant took a knife and slashed Isaac, who responded by knocking the man down with a punch to the head. When you see, as Max did, your old man coming home bleeding, it tends to affect your opinion about the other side of the dispute.

It is the American way, this setting of one group against another while the big boys escape bruises.

In 1931, when longshoremen struck the port in Boston, employers brought in black workers, who were caught in a barrage of rocks and bottles heaved by mostly Irish dock workers in Charlestown.

In 1955, workers striking the Colonial Provision Co. and Boston Sausage Co. in Boston took out an advertisement protesting the use of scabs: "What kind of a job is it where you take the bread and butter off a fellow worker's table?"

As well-paying jobs grow scarce in America, the answer to that forty-year-old question threatens to be, "Just about any job, son."

When times get tough, the tough begin to belt one another around the block. It is a scary prospect.

Workers' average wages have been falling for more than twenty years, when you factor in what the money will buy. In the 1950s, when Max looked with some envy at the pressers and cutters in the garment district plants, about a quarter of the American work force belonged to unions. Now less than 16 percent do.

I'm one of them. I do not mythologize the labor movement. It has had its share of buffoons, leg breakers, communists, incompetents, and corrupt officials. In other words, it is as imperfect as management.

But I'm a union man. I have been on a picket line. I have gone after scabs. I knew firsthand as a kid what it's like when job security and a weekly paycheck suddenly disappear through no fault of the wage earner.

Many in my generation, that of the Silent '50s, held unions in disdain. Many still do. Many could afford to. We were the beneficiaries of the boom years, the likes of which America may never see again. Insecurity now rides high. The middle class is scared, as their working-stiff parents or grandparents were in the old days.

Nowadays, unions—their membership down radically over the years—are doing what businesses have been doing. They are merging into larger operations. I am not smart enough to predict whether that will save the union movement or good jobs for good pay for Americans. But it might level the playing field a bit.

I still walk through what was the garment district. I pass

by the plant where my father picked up his seasonal lines, packed them into big garment bags and stuffed them into the back of his car. Every Saturday, he and the other salesmen would fill up Essex Street, Chauncy Street, Beach Street, Kneeland Street and talk the talk of their trade.

I can hear the echoes as I walk. I can smell the long-gone hot pastrami on rye and chicken noodle soup with matzo balls. I can taste the bourbon, the blended, the Scotch the salesmen preferred before lunch at Dinty Moore's or Warmuth's, now also of blessed memory.

But for all their bravado, all their ability to make it through a blinding blizzard on the way to Bangor, all the strength of forearms it took to lug those sample bags, all the strength of spirit it took to wait patiently for retailers to give them the time of day, for all that, they lacked the security that a union would have given them. And they often were scared, and, sometimes, they would say so.

It was tough to watch men who worked hard since they were kids show and admit to fear. It is just as tough now to hear stories of "downsizing," of the sons and daughters of those old salesmen losing jobs and finding only lower-wage work, if anything.

Samuel Gompers once said, "There are two classes in society, one incessantly striving to obtain the labor of the other class for as little as possible."

It goes on still. So, unlike my father, I have been and remain on this Labor Day weekend a union man.

CHAPTER THREE

What Ever Happened to National Brotherhood Week? Wait . . . It Breathes Yet

My memories of early childhood come neither in technicolor nor in black and white. They are in light brown, preserved in the sepia tones of the old newspaper rotogravure sections. My generation's childhood was framed by World War II. Brown seemed to be the predominant color of our lives.

Army uniforms were brown. Bombers and fighters were often brown. There was that roto section in the paper. And my father's jacket. In style in those times, men wore, if I recall correctly, in their leisure time, fedora hats with short windbreaker jackets. Women wore housedresses. Boys wore long pants whenever they could, even in the thick heat of midsummer, because to wear short pants was to subject oneself to ridicule or worse.

Brown too was the sand at Winthrop Beach, crowded with families, both year-round and summer residents, none of whom knew from swimming pools, vacations, or Cape Cod.

Brown too was the sled on which my father, wearing fedora and jacket, pulled me down the snow-covered street after a winter Nor'easter.

Brown was the two-story house in which we rented the upstairs apartment.

So much for color coordination, a profession that may have existed then but certainly had not reached our neighborhoods.

The other predominant color was white, as in cauca-sian. We knew how to differentiate among white ethnics. In some sections of America, ethnic radar seems to be an inherited gene. There were few blacks on our radar screen. There was one Chinese family, who ran the local laundry. Who knew even the word "Latino" or "Hispanic"? Women in the corporate sector? Hah!

Many speak today of good old days, which existed more in silly television sitcoms for baby boomers than in reality. I deeply believe, albeit with some serious reservations, that we are closer now to the good old days than we were then.

We now struggle openly with the issues of race and class. In those sepia times, we preferred not to think about such things, unless they were thrust in our collective kissers.

Great hypocrisy is attendant upon the attitudes of all peoples on such issues, whatever our race, creed, eth-nicity, or sex. I have written much on Israel and the Middle East, especially when I worked for the *Boston Phoenix,* a weekly paper, but the two *Globe* Israel pieces I include here deal, I hope, with that subject of hypocrisy.

The *Globe* magazine story on the Jewish Defense League is anchored in the political and social atmosphere of the late 1960s and early 1970s. The JDL was threatened by both real and perceived violence and by the often wrenching change that occurs in urban neighborhoods. The JDL straddled that line between self-defense and de-fensiveness that all ethnic and economic classes face.

To struggle with issues of race and class is healthy. Di-versity is not an obscenity. It is an American ideal. And it's a lot more colorful than just brown and white.

Diversity: So What's the Problem?

The scene gladdened the heart of this aging observer, who grew up in a time when you stuck to your own neighborhood and trusted your own kind.

Oh, this area has been a hateful, spiteful place. Too often, our inheritance has been less the love of liberty and more the brunt of bitterness.

But there, in Boston University's Marsh Chapel that night, was a sign of better times, a reflection of how time can wash away wounds, a symbol of what Boston—of what America—can be if we let it, and a reminder of the blessing that whatever we are, we are not Bosnia or the Sudan.

On the altar of this imposing Protestant edifice stood four ushers, each holding a seven-foot-long wooden pole. Attached to the poles was a *chuppah,* a canopy often used in Jewish weddings. The names of the ushers are Molina, Russo, Speliakos, and Waxman. Behind them stood the best man, Powers. All are hyphenated Americans: Molina, Chilean; Russo, Italian; Speliakos, Greek; Waxman, Jewish; Powers, Irish Italian.

The bridesmaids included were another Molina, Protestant, and Lupo, Romanian Russian Jewish, with a healthy dose of Irish and English Catholic and German Lutheran. The bride, Sivits-Alford, is Protestant; the groom, Lupo, is Jewish with the same blood lines as his sister. The clergyman, a rabbi, stood near a table covered with a prayer shawl.

I shall not try the reader's or editor's patience with a description of my son's wedding except where it may be relevant to the point of this offering. And the point is that much maligned word and concept—diversity.

What, exactly, is the problem again?

I keep forgetting. I read criticisms of diversity. I hear

complaints about it. I sometimes kid around myself about the lengths to which some go to ensure a diverse workplace. But I know, for example, that this venerable old rag for which I toil is a far, far better place than it was years ago when everyone pretty much looked and sounded alike.

In the matter of our recent celebration, the diversity came naturally. In other cases, you must nudge it along, even force it at times. Mistakes are made; individuals of all persuasions may be hurt, but the end is a worthy goal. It is nothing short of the American dream that so fascinated earlier observers of this experiment who wondered aloud whether this nation could escape centuries of religious and ethnic warfare so common to other places.

We have not totally escaped, of course. We have suffered from slavery, racism, Indian wars, Know-Nothings, anti-papists, anti-Semites, Klan, Nazi Bund, far-right militias and, time and again, the immigration restrictionists.

The latter are back with us in force. Like those who preceded them in the 1800s and early 1900s, they paint their arguments in attractive hues of economics and even compassion. But too many of them are all about the same business—restrict the outsiders, preserve some perverse version of what an "American" is supposed to be.

For one generation of greater Bostonians, an American was one with English bloodlines, certainly not Irish. For a later generation, an American was only of northern European background, certainly not Italian or Jewish. And so it went, and so it still goes.

Even during my son's wedding, when my heart and mind were rejoicing in our blessing, I thought of the diversity. The writer must never stop thinking of how something might look in print. Who would have stood under the canopy, had the restrictionists succeeded in barring the Irish, Jews, Italians, Greeks and Latin Americans, for example?

The clergyman, Rabbi David Kudan, at one point talked

about the *chuppah*. The sides are open, he said, open to a variety of people who are welcome in one's home.

When my son broke the glass under his foot, Bob Bertram, a Texas-based airline flight attendant with a magnificent voice, sang a Hebrew melody of congratulations. Bob, a Protestant, had spent time making phone calls to cantors in Texas to get the words and pronunciation right.

Those in the pews included elderly Jews whose parents talked in thick accents; Italians who survived the destruction of the West End; Irish, whose ancestors escaped lives of poverty; a dark-skinned Sicilian American, a light-skinned Salvadoran American, a Filipino American, a woman who speaks in a thick Arkansas-Texas accent and whose grandfather had some Indian blood.

Later on, I thought about their faces and voices and rejoiced at the present over the past I had known, a past of looking over one's shoulder, muttering threats against real or illusionary enemies, forging bonds to fight another day, demeaning those who demeaned me and my kind.

So, again I ask. What is the problem here with this diversity?

The Jewish Defense League

Ladies and gentlemen, a statement from the American Jewish Congress:

"The Jewish Defense League is a reckless, irresponsible, extremist group whose violent attitudes and tactics have the same attraction and the same effect as those of the racist groups they claim to oppose. These tactics do not enhance the security of the Jewish community. On the contrary, they serve only to heighten tension, increase hostility and foment panic."

It is Amboy Dukesland. It is East 91st Street between Avenues A and B in East Flatbush, Brooklyn, U.S.A. It is Monday night, and it is snowing, and you are standing, chilled and wet, halfway down the block in front of the Hapoel Hamizrachi Synagogue.

The first cab driver couldn't find East Flatbush, so he deposited you in a Brooklyn cab. The Brooklyn cabbie found East Flatbush and even the street, but he missed the synagogue. You found the synagogue and now you're waiting with instructions to meet a Mr. Polsky, of the Jewish Defense League (JDL), who is going to take you out and look for muggers, rapists, junkies, purse snatchers, and other thugs.

The wind is blowing in from Manhattan, blowing the snow in your face. The snow turns to muddy water as soon as it touches the pavement.

On the way into Brooklyn, the Jewish cabbie was saying, "I just read about them, the Jewish Defense League. They're militant. The other Jewish organizations don't want to be militant with them. Why? You know the Jewish people. They figure if you fight, it'll only get worse. Been turning the other cheek for centuries. We been takin' a bad enough beating as it is. But maybe that's what it takes—a few good beatings."

East Flatbush is urban Jewish, not urbane Jewish à la Jacob Javits, Arthur Goldberg, Ochs-Sulzberger. Urban Jewish, as Dorchester and Mattapan used to be before the kids left their parents in the three-deckers and went south, east, north, west to the split-levels.

The houses are brick red and brown, almost Tudor style, but for working class. Workers, civil servants, their kids, struggling, laughing, fighting, arguing, betting, aggravating, praying in the Borough of Brooklyn. The place is modest. The place is clean. A grandmother walks with her granddaughter around the puddles ("What do you mean, you'll walk alone? A little girl should walk alone at night?") and you hear the fourth police siren in twenty minutes.

Around the corner is a luncheonette on Avenue B. Chopped liver sandwiches cost eighty-five cents, and the milk machine has a picture of Jerry Koosman, of the New York Mets, son of Dodgers, son of God. The counter lady, middle aged, married, no kids, talks, and what she says will anger black readers and pain liberal Jewish readers, but what she says must be written. One must tell it as it appears to be to those who are confused and angry.

"This is a nice neighborhood. (Shrug). But it's changing. The colored are moving in. One Jewish lady and her son, they owned a beautiful old home, near a yeshivah—you're Jewish, aren't you—a yeshivah for girls, a school. The lady lives forty blocks from here, and the son is getting married, so she gave it to a colored broker, and now it's full of colored, right near the yeshivah. (Shake of head). The people are disgusted. They're gonna picket her house, and they're gonna march in on the son's wedding with signs. It's Jewish people doing it to us, our own Jews. You don't find Italians doing that."

A car stops in front of the synagogue, and two faces peer at you. It pulls up to the nearest parking space. Two young men get out.

Sy Polsky, twenty-five, of Brooklyn. A high school teacher,

married a year, his wife expecting, clean cut, neatly dressed. He wears glasses, which he takes off, puts on, takes off, puts on again. He is tall, somewhat thin, and a bit scholarly in appearance.

Gene Keller, seventeen, of Nassau, Long Island. A high school student, adept at the installation, repair, and operation of radios. More emotional than Polsky. Laughs more easily, angers more quickly. A good-looking kid with a blue beret pulled down over a thick thatch of sandy hair, long hair with sideburns, an Army jacket and belt, like the French Resistance. Something on his belt is clacking.

They get a kid from next door to open the synagogue. When they turn on the lights, you see what was clacking. It looks like two billy clubs tied together, end to end, with a black string.

"Nunchukuo," Polsky says. "It's Japanese. Two pieces of solid oak bound by nylon. You can hold one end and swing the other in a circle or figure eight." They practice right in the synagogue, near the Ark that holds the Torah scrolls. Keller tries his karate on Polsky and Polsky ties up Keller's right arm with the nylon and oak. He could break the wrist if he wanted to.

"It's the next most lethal weapon to a gun," Polsky says.

How do you do, Jewish Defense League?

Four more men join Polsky and Keller. Three are teenagers; the other appears to be in his thirties. Three wear yarmulkes. One wears a beret. Some wear the badge ("Never Again . . . Jewish Defense League." The words surround a Star of David).

On the table where the Rabbi normally reads the scriptures, Polsky lays a street map of New York city and a blow-up of East Flatbush. East Flatbush has been divided into three sectors, A, B, and C. Sector A is the worst, because it borders on Ocean Hill–Brownsville.

An ode to Ocean Hill–Brownsville. Oh, the great men who walked your streets and grew up to help mold and share in

the American nightmare . . . Abe Reles . . . the Shapiro broth-
ers . . . Pretty Levine . . . Dasher Abbandando . . . Louis Ca-
pone . . . Pittsburgh Phil . . . Bugsy Goldstein . . . Charlie The
Bug Workman. When Ocean Hill was Italian and Browns-
ville, Jewish, they were tough, and now they're black and
Puerto Rican, and they are tough, and if the Martians move
in next week, the neighborhood will be just as tough. West-
chester, it isn't.

They are getting ready to patrol. JDL is still organizing
its patrols in the neighborhoods. It is too early to tell
whether they are effective. Gene explains how the new radios work. They cost $125 a set, and you can install one
in five minutes or less. Two young men will stay in the
neighborhood. The other four will split up in two cars.

Normally, they explain, there would be three cars, one
per sector, but the local chairman had a dentist appoint-
ment, and, besides, there was an emergency call for JDL
members downtown, where the right-wing National Renaissance Party was supposed to be picketing the Chanukah Festival.

"Remember," Polsky says, "avoid Brownsville. There are
no Jews left there to worry about."

The patrols could avoid Ocean Hill–Brownsville. New
York City cannot. The JDL should pay homage to Ocean
Hill–Brownsville, because that's one of the neighborhoods
where blacks and Puerto Ricans tried to control their
schools and helped prompt a strike in 1968 of the predominantly Jewish teachers' union.

That strike witnessed a most bitter outbreak of anti-
Semitic and anti-black feelings. Liberals writhed in agony.
Oh my God, Jews and blacks are like everyone else, they
learned. They too can hate irrationally. In this ugly setting,
the JDL came forth, if not to prosper, then at least to
persist.

"JDL One, this is JDL Base . . . Over," Keller says into the
speaker. No answer. He tries again.

"What's buggin' me, man? That's not JDL One. That's a gypsy cab driver," in other words, an independent black cabbie who's in business because white cabbies weren't sufficiently servicing black areas. Their radio is stronger than JDL's.

It's snowing and cold. Ergo, it's quiet. "Good," Polsky says.

The patrol skirts Crown Heights. "That's Lincoln Park," Polsky says. "The Great Wisconsin Glacier stopped there."

"Why," he's asked, "was it mugged?"

In Crown Heights, Post 108 of the Jewish War Veterans (their national leadership is against the JDL) gave Rabbi Meir Kahane, JDL founder, a plaque "in sincere appreciation of his absolute devotion ..." Kahane keeps the plaque in his office to beef up his argument that "the people" are with him, even if the leaders aren't.

Chapter Two—*The East Side, Headquarters*

JDL operates out of 156 Fifth Avenue, a nondescript office building on Manhattan's East Side. It's on the third floor, halfway down the corridor from the National Council of American-Soviet Friendship and next door to Cavalcade Books. You knock on the door, which has five locks and a peephole, and Avraham, a young man wearing a white yarmulke, lets you in.

Rabbi Kahane is in a corner office. The offices are small, crowded and separated from one another by cheap plywood partitions. Kahane, thirty-nine, is of medium build, good looking, and conservatively dressed—brown suit, white shirt, brown striped tie, and a black yarmulke that disappears in his dark hair. That's funny, he doesn't look very Jewish. Kahane is funny too, when he's not so deadly serious.

He has just flown in from Montreal, where the French separatists have been making a lot of noise, and some Jews presumably are concerned. But neither he nor his general counsel, Bertram Zweibon, a slightly overweight attorney, will talk about Montreal.

Zweibon has just returned from a press conference, where the JDL asked members of established Jewish organizations to contribute to the JDL half of what they normally would contribute to the other groups. JDL had asked the other groups for $12,500 for patrol equipment. The organizations regard JDL as militant, irresponsible vigilantes and they turned down the request.

At the press conference, Zweibon had to assure reporters that JDL patrols would serve everyone. "If the patrols see a crime committed on the street, they won't run over and say to the victim, 'Are you Jewish?' and then walk away if he isn't."

Kahane's desk is cluttered with papers and envelopes, some of them containing $5 and $10 and $25 donations. ("Dear Rabbi Kahane: Please accept this small contribution to your Worthy cause. Best wishes for continued success. God be with you . . ." an Italian from Brooklyn).

"We're fairly well overdrawn at the bank," Kahane says. "A lot of little five and ten dollar checks come in. No big contributors. They're afraid to be in any way linked to us because of the hatchet job done to us."

So it begins. Stories of persecution, some real, some imagined. The theories and philosophy of JDL. Kahane and Zweibon have written and said things that are repeated almost word for word in East Flatbush, Philadelphia, Newton. This in paraphrase is how they feel.

Established Jewish organizations are out of touch with the Jews on the street. Mayor Lindsay is selling out the Jews because of black and Puerto Rican pressure; other civil authorities may do likewise. The police have been told to go easy on rioters. Special exemptions for minorities in civil service and college admissions are discrimination in reverse. Jews are not "patsies" and will no longer be pushed around. The Extreme Left will push the Great Silent Middle into the Extreme Right, and Democracy will suffer, and the Jews will suffer the most. We are not vigilantes—we stop criminals; we do not prosecute or execute them. We are not racists. That's the theory. Here is some of the practice.

When an SDS chapter seized an administration office at Brooklyn College, the JDL threatened to go down about 6 P.M. and pull them out physically.

When the Nazi-like National Renaissance Party did some anti-Semitic picketing, the JDL went down and began busting heads. "We left eight of them on the sidewalk," Kahane says proudly.

When black activist James Forman was scheduled to appear at the fashionable temple Emanu-El on Fifth Avenue and demand reparations, JDL appeared with chains and bats, much to the distress of the temple's rabbi. Forman did not show, but reportedly had changed his mind anyway.

"The established Jewish organizations don't want the public to hear our messages," Kahane reasons, "because of the old ghetto fear that groups such as ours will cause anti-Semitism. They're timid Jews who don't want Jews to be too visible. Jews should stop worrying about being loved. We should start demanding the same respect other human beings are demanding. Forget about love. You can't get love without respect, and there's no respect without self respect."

Hey, Kahane, you sound like advocates of black power and pride.

"Well, they're one hundred percent right. Black nationalism is long overdue, self-pride, self-respect. But we object to it becoming Naziism, the hatred of others. We have nothing but the highest praise for those black leaders whose love of people gets them on the streets to demand what's rightfully theirs."

The rhetoric is not bad but it sometimes belies the reality. For what Kahane means by "what's rightfully theirs" and what blacks mean could be two different things.

Kahane recalls proudly how he turned down offers of cooperation from Anthony Imperiale, Newark's karate-chopping Italo-American vigilante, because he won't work with anyone who says "nigger." But yelling "nigger" is not the only sign of a racist, and you come away feeling the JDL is not the most sensitive organization when it comes to understanding the black revolution.

When you tell Kahane that some blacks are trying to crack down on pimps and pushers in their neighborhoods, he says "great" and then you ask him if JDL will crack down on Jewish slumlords, and he says, "No, they should be handled by the courts."

You are a Jew covering Jews and now you know a little more what it's like for a black covering blacks. Maybe, the reporter's all-American reaction is to put down the militant but deep down you are proud that your own kind are protecting your own kind.

That is . . . to protect from a real threat. To patrol streets and work with the police. To protect a shul from vandalism. But to stand in front of a synagogue because someone is coming with a demand with which you disagree? Is this protection or provocation?

What makes for a Jewish Defense League?

To begin with, it is not new, this phenomenon. The Bible has precedents. The Palestine underground. The London defense groups that organized against street thugs in Stepney. The protective leagues in Russia. The gangs in your childhood.

Maybe there is a JDL for the same reason that young Russian Jews are wearing Moshe Dayan buttons and proclaiming "Ich bin a Yid" (I am a Jew). Maybe some Jews who see televised accounts of riots recall the breakdown of society in Germany before the Holocaust.

Maybe it's racism. Maybe it's a political reaction against the growing power and demands of other minorities. Maybe it's even a way of rediscovering yourself.

A number of Jews, as their black counterparts, are telling everyone they will not be pushed around. So the JDL
runs a Summer camp in the Catskills to teach karate and
street fighting and Jewish culture. It requires all members
to learn karate and urges them to buy guns.

So what does all this mean for the street Jew and the
establishment Jew?

Chapter Three—*Lower East Side, Two Views*

In that pocket of Yiddish culture left on the Lower East
Side, home of the Jewish press and the Yiddish theater,
where the *Daily Forward* editor smokes his cigarette conti-
nental style and whose English is accented more European
than Yiddish, where the writers dine two doors down at
the Tel Aviv Restaurant and drink mineral water, in that
block surrounded by all the tragedy of the "other" Lower
East Side . . .

"It makes the Jewish community vulnerable, when someone adopts the posture that Jews need this kind of attention and defense." This is William Stern, slight, white-
haired administrative director of The Workmen's Circle,
housed in the *Daily Forward* building. Stern says what Kahane criticizes his critics for saying.

"It means Jews regard themselves as being a special
group in the community. We don't want to isolate ourselves . . . so the violator will not just see white, he will
see Jew. There's nothing wrong with protecting a synagogue but to stand offensively with weapons is itself a
provocation. It appears like a declaration of war, and that's
the worst thing of all.

"As soon as the Jewish community declares war, it's
communal suicide. The objective of the organized Jewish
community is to moderate differences, to create a bridge
of understanding . . . the JDL could do serious harm to the
Jewish community, which has reason to think of itself as

having advanced the cause of civil rights and community harmony. They will have the opposite effect."

Yet, a number of Jews are being turned off by some aspects of liberalism. In other words, you can build bridges but you need strong supports. You need the Jakes. You've got to convince people like Jake (last name declined), who lived the first seventeen of his eighteen years on the Lower East Side, who learned street fighting and then taught it to JDL campers.

"JDL believes Jews should fight back," Jake says. He is standing on the corner, not far from The Forward building. "The B'nai B'rith and the rest of them don't seem to be able to come down and do something for the man on the street. What have they done for the man in the Lower East Side? Yet they'll give money to black organizations who hate us."

Maybe Jake has some facts wrong but one thing Jake knows very well is the feel of a fist in his face, hard enough to knock the yarmulke off his head. So the Jakes have joined JDL, and they aren't the only ones.

Chapter Four—*Newton, Mass.*

"Right," Alan Mandel agrees, "you have to treat the causes of crime, not just the effects, but while you're treating the causes, how many persons do you allow to be beaten up?"

Mandel, bearded and broad-shouldered, sits with four other men in an expensive modern house in Newtonville. The floors are carpeted wall to wall. The dining room table is neatly set with coffee cups and pastries. Three children have been put to bed. Their mother is baking a pie in the kitchen.

Mandel is an engineer from Brookline and chairman of the JDL Boston branch. Marvin Antelman, rabbi and chemist, is the host and New England regional coordinator for the JDL. Dr. David Love, older than the others, is an engineer from Newton. A fourth man, unidentified, is a mathematician from Brookline. The fifth is Irv Jacobsen, of Newton, also an engineer.

Five pleasant, educated men. The scene looks like a meeting of some temple's brotherhood committee. Yet they are talking about hand-to-hand combat and the use of bats.

So now, JDL is here. Maybe it doesn't have seven thousand members, as it claims. And it probably isn't well organized in too many places.

But it is beginning to organize patrols in Mattapan and Dorchester to protect the elderly, and it has stood in front of Temple Emanuel in Newton (uninvited) to prevent a tenants organization from disrupting the bar mitzvah of the son of a controversial landlord (the tenants, already negotiating with the landlord, weren't coming anyway).

Eighteen of them stand in front of the synagogue.

"I think it's wonderful," a woman says five times.

"Who asked for you?" an old man yells. "Who needs you?"

"Where can we send a check?" another woman asks.

"Idiots," a man mutters.

So go make a conclusion.

There is no conclusion. The JDL was inevitable. History has created it, and history will judge it. It is a response to a need for security. It is a manifestation of virility, self assertion, pride. Maybe it's racism.

Perhaps, at least, a suggestion is in order, a very idealistic suggestion perhaps. Even in Mattapan, victims of crime are not only Jewish. If civilian patrols are necessary, should they be Jewish or black?

Do we need a fully integrated patrol, one that will not only try to stop incidents of purse snatchings and muggings but also address itself to the well-known causes of such crimes?

On Woodrow Avenue, where the fathers of the Jewish

chemists and engineers and mathematicians lived, is the office of Youth, Inc. Its chairman is Thomas Arnold. He is twenty-eight years old and black. He too is a chemist, and he is worried that a JDL will only provoke trouble among young blacks.

Before we all become witness to some insanity, is it not possible that the chemists of Woodrow Avenue and the chemists of Newtonville could start talking to each other?

So that for black and Jews, one can truly pledge "Never Again"?

So that every night will be as peaceful as that snowy night in East Flatbush, where Polsky said, "Good, every night should be like this."

Today I Am a Fountain Penski

It should have been a time of tranquility and good will. But the fundamentalists had their own agenda.

Eric Strom, thirteen, of Stamford, Connecticut, was celebrating his bar mitzvah in a Crakow, Poland, synagogue. His was the first bar mitzvah held there in twenty years.

The boy's ancestors, Polish Jews, had told him of the fate of Jews in such places. Once, Crakow was home to sixty thousand Jews. Today, the average age of the few Jews in Crakow is in the seventies. No wonder their leader cried openly in joy and in pain as this American boy celebrated his entry into Jewish manhood.

But sitting with the kid was an uninvited guest, Rabbi Nachum Elbaum, who runs a travel agency that organizes bar mitzvahs for American Jews in Jerusalem. He said he was there representing Orthodox groups, which raised a stink.

And why did they raise a stink?

Because the rabbi who was to officiate at the ceremony was Rabbi Emily Korzenick, who had tutored the kid and accompanied the family to Crakow. That first name is not Emil, or Emile, or Elmer, but Emily, as in woman, not man, so for the Orthodox, why the very heavens were rent asunder.

A woman rabbi? Among the Orthodox, women are not even allowed to pray with the men. They sit in the back of the bus. That is precisely where Rabbi Emily Korzenick spent most of the ceremony—up in the balcony of the synagogue.

When the bar mitzvah boy called her down to join him and read the remarks she had prepared—remarks condemning violence and intolerance—Rabbi/Travel Agent Elbaum pulled Rabbi Korzenick's prayer shawl away and then interrupted her several times as she spoke.

The Polish Jews were embarrassed by such goings-on, but they had not at all been upset at Rabbi Korzenick's role.

I am upset, however.

I am upset at the Orthodox Jews who behave so foolishly, so intolerantly. I am upset at the Pope and his conservative advisers who still insist that priests must be celibate and that no women must ever be priests.

I am upset at Muslim fundamentalists who stand ready to topple moderate governments in the name of Allah. I am upset at American Protestant fundamentalists who defy the very brains that God gave them and insist on taking the Bible at its word.

Who in God's name are such people to offend the very dignity of humankind by asserting that they have a monopoly on morality, that they alone have cornered the market on God?

This is who they are: they are groups of politically potent persons who want to keep their power. If you, an individual, wish to pray, they imply, you must play and pay. You must play by their rules and pay for that with your ability to think for yourself.

God must have a good sense of humor to put up with such goings-on, to watch each group of fundamentalists run around, waving its own version of the rule book and screaming, "No *this* is the true way."

It reminds me of the parochial school teams about to compete. Each team would kneel and pray, thereby giving God the impossible task of deciding whether St. Michael's or St. Gregory's deserved the better jump shots.

But it really is not very funny, not when you try to estimate the millions who have died in the name of organized religion, whether the religion was that pledging fealty to God or that kneeling at the altar of some economic or political ideology.

The fundamentalists attack atheistic communism as a

perversion of freedom, all the while denying equal rights to their own kind. The fundamentalist communists attack organized religion as oppressive, but would persecute those who stray from the party line.

They are all a joke. My fantasy is that all the fundamentalist rabbis, priests, mullahs, and ministers, along with the sloganeering communists, be gathered together and be given their own nation-state.

Let them live together and bicker to their hearts' content. As a Jew, I am inclined to name their nation Chelm. This is the fictional village of the old folk tales. It is a village of fools.

From Russia with Hate

When I read the words tumbling out of the mouth of the Russian ultranationalist Vladimir Zhirinovsky, I figured it could be worse. I could be reading such claptrap in Minsk, or Odessa, or Moscow, rather than in the safety of Greater Boston.

So, I concluded, it was once again time to bless three persons who had the smarts and courage to get out of Russia around the turn of the century, thereby creating a chain of circumstances that enabled me to be born here.

Sometimes, "here" has not been such a wonderful place, what with gang fights, bigotry, unemployment, crime, corruption, ignorant voters, homogenized culture, and dollar worship.

Indeed, the three Russian grandparents and the grandfather from Romania—also a very good place to leave—had their share of *tsouris*, which is Yiddish for bad luck or aggravation. But a really lousy day in America has proven often to be better than a pretty good day in Minsk or Pinsk.

Zhirinovsky, whose illogically named Liberal Democratic Party has gained power in Russia's new parliament, said recently, "We are not anti-Semites, but our voters have asked us to change things. They don't like non-Russian announcers on TV, so they have asked us to remove them and replace them with good Slavic faces." It is the Jews who provoke anti-Semitism, he noted.

Aha! Where have we heard that before? The answer is: throughout history. The answer for extra points is: often in Russia and its immediate neighbors or satellites. And the lesson is? Grab the samovar, the feather pillows and the candlesticks, and do a Saconovitz or a Krupnick, which is to say, leave.

Saconovitz had been the name of my mother's parents

before they or somebody changed it to Sacon. Krupnick had been the name of my father's mother before she met Isaac Lupescu, late of Romania, in the East End of London, married him and journeyed here. As Saconovitz became Sacon, Lupescu became Lupo. Only in America, such miracles.

Not that it was easy to leave Russia, or anyplace else. It wasn't as if you were just walking away from a house or a village. You were leaving behind family, friends, and your whole history, your culture, all that you had been for centuries.

Grandpa Saconovitz had served in the cavalry. My mother would later say that he was so strong he could lift a horse off the ground. But in the Russian military, the Jews were generally fed after the horses. We do not know if he deserted, or how he got out, but get out he did, all the way to New York City, first, and then to Chelsea, and he made enough money to send for his wife, Rose, a Minsk dressmaker and daughter of a talmudic scholar.

In America, not only could your names change, but also your fortunes. We are speaking here not of fortunes, as in money, but, rather, of the more important meaning, to wit, health and the length of one's life. And, what's more, you could continue to speak in Yiddish, pray in Hebrew and sit in the warmest room of a Chelsea tenement—the kitchen—and talk with old friends about the old country.

Sometimes, their sons and daughters listened. More often, they were too busy becoming Americans. And we grandchildren are left with a sepia photo or two, some musty memories and much confusion about who left when and who arrived when.

In the fortune-as-money category, neither the Sacon nor the Lupo immigrants nor most of their offspring did particularly well. At times, each grandfather worked in the *shmateh* trade, Sacon as a presser and Lupo as a trimmer and cutter.

And they had problems in a few other categories as well, as did many immigrant families, popular American folk history to the contrary notwithstanding.

The partners in both sets of grandparents separated. Grandpa Sacon went deaf early in life, became quite frustrated as a result of that and died too early to get to know his grandchildren. Grandpa Lupo worked only occasionally and died before most of his grandchildren were born. My father would later recall of his family, "a lot of fights, everybody pulling away from everybody else."

Most of their offspring didn't get to go to college, but all their grandchildren would have that opportunity. This too was a miracle, for it might not have happened in Mother Russia. Another miracle is not what did happen, but, rather, what did not happen. We did not get killed. For here is a brief description of what transpired back home in the Minsk area after the Saconovitzs left:

On May 26, 1905, Russian soldiers and Cossacks carried out a pogrom against the Jews. The fact that Grandpa Sacon had been in the Tsar's cavalry probably would have counted for nothing. On October 18, pogroms broke out all over Russia. In Minsk, forty-two Jews were killed and several hundred wounded. In other words, I could have been wiped out before I started.

On October 21, 1943, after three years of rounding up and killing Jews, the Nazis put the finishing touches on the Minsk ghetto and wiped out its two thousand remaining residents. Jews had lived in Minsk since the 1300s. That day, I was a pretty nervous kid, because first grade had me quite confused—as would grades two through twelve—but confused at age five is better than dead at age five.

Had family members somehow survived all that, we might have been treated to Stalin-sponsored hits or the tender mercies of the secret police. And, finally, were—or are—there any family members left, they could sit in their somber gray apartments and watch Vladimir Zhirinovsky on television, a medium that he would expunge of Jewish announcers.

The Russian grandfather realized few of his dreams in America. But this grandson, who remembers the man only vaguely, thanks him effusively. Good move, *zeydeh*.

Is There a Double Standard for Jews?

It seems that after a couple of millennia, we Jews are suddenly tough guys. I guess if you wait around long enough, anything can happen, and, believe me, it has been a long wait.

When I was younger, I was informed that the reason America had to fight World War II was because Jews couldn't defend themselves. "Jews are chicken," I was told, and the Jews who were in the service were not doing any fighting. In Dorchester and Roxbury, in Winthrop and Revere, Jews were people you could make fun of by faking a Yiddish accent. Jews were international capitalists and insidious communists. And, of course, Jews could not play sports.

Beyond that were the charges of deicide, sabbath bloodletting and general, all-purpose treason, which had triggered hundreds of pogroms for centuries.

So, as you might guess, it has been quite a job, this being Jewish, what with starting whole wars we decide not to fight in, and putting up those fake stars of David in military cemeteries, and making millions of dollars every week to sponsor commie revolutions, and convincing people like Sandy Koufax and Hank Greenberg and Sid Luckman to pretend to be Jewish athletes and squishing all those red and white blood cells out of unsuspecting gentile children. With all that work, you're lucky to get a weekend to yourself.

Those days seem like yesterday, though if you acknowledge that anti-Semitism never really goes away, those days seem like today. Did you know, for example, that there may have been no Holocaust? Or that I, as a Jew, may be responsible for some Midwestern family losing its farm? I'll tell you something else about being Jewish—every day is an education.

But, that aside, how did it happen so quickly that we went from craven to brazen, from cowardly to aggressive? Did we actually sip or bake into our matzoh some of that non-Jewish blood, as alleged long ago by czarist Russians or more recently by a Syrian government official? Or is it just possible that, all along, we've been like everybody else? That we produce heroes and cowards and a lot of folks somewhere in between, just as Christians, Moslems, Buddhists, and agnostics have done?

That is why Israel is so damn important to us, because it is a nation, like all nations, full of the good and bad, the extraordinarily pious and the morally outrageous. Now, perhaps finally, we can say to other religions, races, clans, tribes and nations essentially what Shylock asked rhetorically: if you cut me, pal, you think I don't also bleed?

Understand that in Israel, young soldiers, untrained for riot control, behave pretty much as did American national guardsmen during the black riots of the 1960s and at Kent State. Note that just as southern Baptists and Middle East Muslims have their share of closed-minded fundamentalists, there are in Israel Jewish Jimmy Swaggarts who think the Bible is a collection of zoning ordinances for the West Bank and Gaza.

Being like everyone else works both ways, that is, for those who criticize us and for ourselves.

Fellow American Jews say that they are sick at heart over the violence in the occupied territories, but ask why the media concentrate so much on such pictures? Are we being singled out again? I hope not. I hope it's because it's news. The real question is why the media and others who purport to care do not give equal play to the Chinese repression in Tibet, the persecution of Coptic Christians in Egypt, the human rights violations in Arab states, North Korea, Czechoslovakia, Indonesia, Guatemala, and Vietnam. If one used television coverage as a guide, one would think that unrest had come to a virtual halt in South Africa.

And the media also mistakenly figure it is also no longer news to note repeatedly that for many Arabs, the only good Israel is a dead Israel.

To Israel's dilemma, there are answers, ranging from training troops in riot control to negotiating over the occupied territories. But to even our most sympathetic critics who have not an anti-Semitic bone in their bodies, I, who regard Israeli West Bank behavior and policy as dumb and dangerous, have an answer too:

Never again will we be victims, hoping that righteous gentiles will save us from Nazis, that caring Palestinians will shield us from rioters, or that well-meaning American school teachers will chide gentile kids to be nice to Jewish kids. If it is our fate to be either victim or aggressor, I opt for the second. I keep praying for multiple choice.

Those Who Judge Israel

Who will judge Israel?

To pose the question is in no way to excuse Israel's excesses, to defend all of its internal and external policies, to legitimize its fundamentalists. Israel, as any country, must stand up to scrutiny. It just seems that Israel seems to get scrutiny wholesale.

On page 11 of the *Globe* one day were the headlines "Skulls in Fields, Corpses in Church: Legacies of Liberia's Reign of Terror" and "Train Torched in Indian Strife— Death Toll 47." Not page 1, page 11. A week later, on page 8 of the *New York Times* was the headline "18 Killed in Muslim-Hindu Clash as Politician's Arrest Is Protested." Not page 1, page 8.

Where are the front-page accounts of State Department angst, or United Nations anger, or international disapproval when Tamil guerrillas in Sri Lanka carry out pogroms on Muslims? Or when Afghan militants attack relief workers? Or when Islamic Jihad in the Gaza Strip calls for "a revolution of knives against the millions of Soviet Jews arriving" in Israel?

Will Malawi judge Israel? Last March, the police of this southern African nation shot and killed twenty protesters after citizens stoned an armed convoy. Africa Watch, a human rights organization, reported, "Although many states in sub-Saharan Africa suffer from greater political violence than Malawi, there are fewer African countries with such a combination of totalitarianism and personal despotism."

How about Zaire? Will Zaire judge Israel? In August, the Lawyers Committee for Human Rights blamed that government for a "systematic pattern of abuses," including beatings, crackdowns on political opponents and free speech, and arbitrary arrests.

Will Malaysia judge Israel? From May 1989 to July of this

year, that nation rejected more than 8,700 Vietnamese refugees, or about 90 percent of those who sought asylum there.

Or let Japan, that paragon of racial insensitivity, judge. Various Japanese officials have blamed American social and economic problems on blacks, Puerto Ricans, and Mexicans. As for Japan's disdain for other Asians, ask the Chinese or the Koreans.

There's always Great Britain. The British, who carved up Palestine and turned it into something now called Jordan, have a long and less than illustrious history in meddling in the affairs of others. For years, the Brits have run Hong Kong. In 1997, they'll turn it over to China, another state of extraordinary virtue. When it was suggested that Britain take in 50,000 Hong Kong families, 65 percent of the British said no. Perhaps the Hong Kong natives should consider themselves fortunate; 83 percent of the Brits opposed more immigrants from India, Pakistan, and the West Indies, and 67 percent didn't want more Jews.

Will Spain and France judge Israel? Perhaps the Arab and North African immigrants in both those nations would also welcome a United Nations force in Madrid and Marseilles to deter natives from assaulting immigrants.

Romanians who attack ethnic Hungarians could judge, or perhaps Serbs who assault ethnic Albanians, or those Bulgarian Slavs who detest ethnic Turks.

If the United Nations should set off to investigate Israel, perhaps it could make a quick stop in Lebanon to learn how many Christians the Syrians killed in the most recent stifling of a rebellion. Or it could try to condemn publicly the eighty deaths two months ago in the Ein Hilweh refugee camp, where Yasser Arafat's troops went after Abu Nidal's loyalists.

Does the endless Hindu-Muslim conflict within India and between India and Pakistan qualify those nations to sit in judgment of Israel? How about Guatemala, with its putrid

human rights record? Or El Salvador, where you can sometimes have a whole lunch without being in the middle of a
firefight?

Or maybe the United States, which occupies the territory of the Arapaho, Sioux, Seminole, Iroquois, Mohawk,
Ute, Navajo, Comanche, and the Mexicans, could lecture
Israel on the West Bank and Gaza, without which Israel is
nine and a half miles wide in its middle.

No, Israel's excesses will find no defense here, but neither will international hypocrisy.

The Good Old Days Are Now: Well, Mostly

We cannot dwell always on the past. Even we Jews, blessed and plagued with institutional memories, must look around and give thanks for the present.

As the Irish Americans say, "I woke up this morning on the right side of the ground."

As Gerry Burke, one of three brothers who run Doyle's, a real saloon in Boston's Jamaica Plain neighborhood, reminds me often, "These are the good old days, my friend."

Indeed, they are, which is not to say I fail to grieve over the lost poetry of my past. Were that the case, I should not have written many of these pieces.

We must figure out how to preserve the past and enjoy the present. As for planning for the future, I'll leave that to the accountants and the investment counselors, and I won't even blame them should there be another Depression.

I am the only one of four generations of my family to remain in our community. The fourth generation, our son and daughter, have gone off to find love and their dreams elsewhere.

They and their contemporaries are the present and the future. They comprise our new "good old days," so as I celebrate the old-timers, I celebrate the newcomers too.

Ahead of Her Time for Going On-Line

About a half century ago, Esther Sacon Lupo, my very own mother, went on line to do her grocery shopping. She clearly was ahead of her time.

Look how long it took big business to catch up. Only now do I read in the paper that Stop & Shop is going to provide on-line grocery service to Greater Boston. For five bucks a month, you get the opportunity to order food or whatever on your computer. When they deliver the stuff, you pay them another five bucks plus 5 percent of the grocery bill.

Not only was my mother ahead of her time technologically, but also economically. I'll explain:

It is, say, 1946, and it is raining. Pouring, actually. So my mother, who does not drive, calls our grocer, Kaplow's Creamery, which is about a dozen blocks from our apartment, and talks to one of the Kaplows. By the way, they are also our landlords, which may not have meant anything on line, but certainly gave us an inside line on what was fresh that day.

"Hello, Fanny?" my mother is saying. "Did Izzy get smelts today? Good, you'll give me a dozen smelts. And three potatoes. Max is coming home from the road tonight. And peas. You got peas? Some peas. And I need butter, you'll send some butter . . ."

At the other end of this high-tech process, Fanny Kaplow is writing this down on a piece of paper you use to wrap fish, or on a paper bag. Next to each item, she marks the price. And, lo and behold, later in the day, a small panel truck pulls up to the front of the two-story house, and out comes a high school kid, who walks upstairs with a box in his hands, and if there's any spare change in the house, he gets a few cents—he gets a lot less than ten bucks plus 5 percent of the total bill.

This same technology is used to order meat from Al Bramson, the kosher butcher.

"Al, you got some nice *flunken* today?" Esther asks on her hardware, a black phone with a rotary dial. "Not too fatty, Al. Last time was too fatty."

At his end, Al, equally proficient in technology, answers, "You can't have *flunken* without fat, Esther. *Flunken* has fat. Without the fat, there's no taste. Last time, you told me there was no taste."

Back to our end. "Taste is good. But fat is no good. A little fat is OK. I don't want too fat. I'll send the boy back if it's too fat."

At Al's end, a sigh is heard on line. "Oy, all right. I'll send you *flunken* with fat, but not too much fat. What else?"

I ask you techno-nerds, you yuppified shoppers, will you be able to engage in such dialogue when you go on-line with the supermarket?

Neither Esther, nor Fanny, nor Al is around anymore. They've all gone to the great grocery in the sky, from where they are looking down at us, nodding knowingly and saying, "Nu? A big deal, on-line. You want technology? We did technology. A phone, a pencil, and a paper bag. And no five bucks a month, either."

Acting to Make Parents Proud

Early in the mornings, Alyssa would awaken and begin her monologues. In stream-of-consciousness baby talk, she would address stuffed animals, including an assortment of dogs and bears and a blue pig.

My wife and I would laugh as quietly as we could and listen to what undoubtedly were some of the great lines of babydom. Unlike her brother, who had shown no patience for remaining in a crib and had busted out as soon as the wardens had turned their backs, she could lie there for an hour and talk gibberish.

Now she is a quarter century old. She still delivers lines.

"Wisdom! To leave his wife, to leave his babes, his mansion and his titles, in a place from whence himself does fly? He loves us not. He wants the natural touch. For the poor wren, the most diminutive of birds, will fight, her young ones in her nest, against the owl."

No child blabbering in the dawn there; no, that is Lady Macduff, dressed all in white and cuddling to her body an infant, venting anger at her missing husband, all the while preparing to verbally joust with her young son and, soon, to be garrotted and drowned by Macbeth.

For maybe two seconds, my wife and I are no longer audience members, but again parents. I am thinking briefly of putting out a contract on Jonathan Epstein. Sure, he is doing a wonderful Macbeth, but couldn't he have let her off with just a warning?

Cribs and gibberish are long gone now, packed away in that corner of the heart and that attic of the mind that every parent holds as storage for the memories of his or her children's childhood. Her stage is now a real stage; her audience more discriminating than stuffed bears and dogs and a blue pig.

Alyssa has been an actress for a long time now, but each

time we see her and her colleagues perform, we marvel as both parents and audience at what actors can do. We are not theater critics, but, yuk, yuk, we know what we like. More to the point, we know when we are touched deep in the soul.

On this day, she does two roles in a midday performance of *Hamlet* and five roles in an evening performance of *Macbeth*. That comes with the territory at Shakespeare & Company—that, and playing in the sometimes stifling heat of the stables down the dirt road from Edith Wharton's Lenox mansion.

As Gertrude, she is poisoned in *Hamlet;* as Lady Macduff, she is choked and drowned in *Macbeth*. Toe-tapping musical comedy it ain't.

"The reviews have been good," she told us one day on the phone, "but the plays are murdering me."

We wonder—how does anyone play seven roles in one day, or two roles. If truth be told, we wonder how anyone plays any role.

They are professionals, these actors. Once upon a time, as kids, they might have started out playing at it, but not for long. They took to it. They're the ones who might not have had the lead roles in high school or college but who had the passion for this job that demands so much and pays so little.

I never knew and still cannot fully fathom how much physical, mental, and emotional energy is required for this profession of hers. I never knew about the voice exercises, which sometimes approach the old baby gibberish, or about the training in stage combat, or the relaxation techniques.

My acting career began as a teenager in front of the bathroom mirror and ended in college fraternity shticks. My wife did college musicals and still tries show tunes when environmental police are not around and about. My son, the cop, can do many things, but they do not include singing, for which perpetrators can be thankful, as it would constitute cruel and unusual punishment.

So, well-meaning people say, oh, she must get it from her parents, but no. She gets it from within herself. Oh, there are bits and pieces actors can pick up from their families—some mannerisms here, some voice inflections there—but the raw talent is their own, as is the lifetime of strenuous work it takes to hone that talent.

At the end of *Hamlet,* as Horatio promises to tell "the yet unknowing world . . . of carnal, bloody and unnatural acts, of accidental judgments, casual slaughters, of deaths put on by cunning and forced cause," I am reduced to tears. At the end of *Macbeth,* I can barely speak.

When she comes out from backstage to join us, it is clear she and her colleagues have been self-critical again. They are their own toughest critics.

"Tell me honestly now," she says, "was it really all right?"

Oh, I tell you, kid, it was and remains much more than all right.

My Son the Cop

"Boston police officer shot dead; suspect held . . . R. I. officer on trail of robbers is killed . . . Paxton police chief is gunned down . . ." Boston Globe *headlines during the past week.*

Wherever I go in my house, I see the remnants of an earlier era. On the first floor, on the wall to the left as I face up the stairs, is a composite of photos taken when my son and daughter were at various stages of being just kids. In one I am holding my son, about a year or so old, and he is staring over my shoulder at whatever attracted the attention of this pudgy-faced child.

He is twenty-seven now. The round cheeks and little pot tummy of childhood are but photos on the wall and in the mind's eye of memory. He is tall, broad-shouldered and strong in mind, spirit, and body. My son is a cop.

In the third-floor hallway leading to my office at home is a pile of stuffed animals, survivors from many a staged play or slapstick combat scene. Once in a while, I'll pat one on the head, both to let the animals know that they haven't been forgotten and to reassure myself that I can somehow reach out through them and still protect my kids.

If you are any kind of parent, you spend a lot of time and mental energy worrying about your kids, and that means worrying about things that you often cannot control. And just when you think you are finished with worrying about childhood diseases, sports accidents, local bullies, drug dealers, and "I'm taking the car," you discover new genres of concerns.

My daughter, the actress, must drive on snow-slicked roads in the Berkshires or take late-night subway rides in New York City. The woman with whom my son lives needs foot surgery. Her daughter gets an infection.

And my son is a cop.

"A series of unprovoked ambushes on police officers in Los Angeles has cops jittery and has prompted Police Chief Willie Williams to order all patrollers who don't already do so to work in pairs."—Law Enforcement News

My son seems to be a very able cop. His reflexes are good. He brings both street smarts and book smarts to the job. He has enough self confidence that he doesn't try to cover up a mistake. He can take down a perpetrator, fire a weapon, talk sense to the unruly and master the chaos of rules, regulations, laws, and paperwork that confront police officers daily.

My wife and I are as proud of him being a cop as we are of his sister being an actress. I guess when we asked them as children what they wanted to be, and they answered, as so many kids do, "policeman" and "actress," they actually meant it. Good for them.

"Do you worry?" some friends ask.

Most of the time, no. You can't, or you destroy yourself inside. If you worry too much, you unintentionally emit that scent when you talk to your kid, and that's bad for his morale.

So, we tell him what we really feel, which is the truth. We tell him to be careful, as if he needed us to tell him that. We tell him that we are proud and that he is good, that he's got all the right instincts for the job, that we trust his judgment.

And then I read the papers.

"An off-duty police officer who joined fellow officers in chasing a driver in a stolen car was killed Monday night in Queens when the suspect's vehicle crashed into the officer's car at over 70 miles per hour."—New York Times

Or I'll watch the televised funeral of a cop and hear the keening of the bagpipes. The Irish, God love them, have left many a mark on policing, and the wail of the pipes is symbolically the most gut-wrenching of them.

My eyes well up in tears; my heart seems to drop deep

into my gut, and some long-ago response from the Army overtakes me, and I sometimes stand, my right arm crooked, the fingers of my right hand stretched out and knitted together as one, and I salute.

And now, because my son is a cop, I say a little prayer, a very selfish prayer for which I make no apologies. "Dear God, don't let those pipes ever be for him."

My boy is a tall, strong, athletic, handsome, smart kid, a quick study. He could have chosen any field. He said he wanted the excitement of law enforcement. And he said he wanted to get the bad guys off the streets.

On Fridays, he and Connie, his loved one, go to the local elementary school kindergarten in the Texas town where they live and join Connie's daughter, age five, for lunch. They bring Happy Meals from McDonald's. And then he goes home, gets into a uniform and body armor, straps on a nine-millimeter handgun, and goes to work.

I called him to tell him that I was writing this. I owe him that. I asked him if he felt he was helping people.

"Absolutely," he said. "Somebody's got to do it. People have to have someone they can turn to."

Does he regret his decision?

"Not at all."

For what it's worth to him and all his brother and sister officers, neither do we.

Noblesse Obliges Him to Forgo
the Throne

I am announcing today that I, Alan Lupo, grandson of the Lupescus and a totally illegitimate heir-in-law to the Romanian throne, hereby renounce any and all claims to that throne even if it becomes available following recent bloody events there.

I don't want it. I don't need it. I wouldn't look at it. I wouldn't sit on it if they gave it to me.

If King Michael, the exiled Romanian monarch living in Switzerland, wants to return to Bucharest to head up a constitutional monarchy, as he says he does, good luck to him. I want to reassure him that I shall not contest him for it, though I have to wonder why anyone in his right mind would leave Switzerland for anyplace. I, on the other hand, would be leaving only Winthrop, if I were going, which I am not.

Michael, now sixty-eight, is the son of the late King Carol and his second wife, the princess Helene. I am supposedly a distant relative of the late Magda Lupescu, who replaced Helene as what we might now politely call Carol's main spouse equivalent.

Magda's father was supposed to have been Jewish. Some say he changed his name from Wolff to Lupescu, which is Romanian for "wolf." He did this in order to blend into a society that was not noted for its love of Jews. This may have made more sense than the move by my father's father or someone in his family to change the name Lupescu to Lupo, which is Italian for "wolf." If this was their idea of blending into America, they booted it.

Magda's pop was either a pharmacist, saloon owner, junk dealer, money lender, or middleman in some kind of vague commercial transactions. How he made a living depends on who was telling the story, but at least he made a living, something that my grandfather Lupo (nee Lupescu) rarely managed to do because he didn't like working much.

Anyway, my grandfather told his children that they were all related to Magda, the attractive, brilliant mistress to King Carol. This was quite a notion here in America and its mention turns many a head. Had we been still in Romania, we would have kept our mouths shut because all sorts of Romanians, including students, peasants, and Nazis, kept threatening to kill Magda. Come to think of it, had we still been in Romania, we probably would have been dead.

Romanians resented Magda not only for being half Jewish, which she denied, but also for having attracted Carol away from his royal wife, for allegedly manipulating the government, for making some smart financial deals for herself and so on. She was blamed for just about anything that was going wrong in Romania from the late 1920s up to World War II.

She and Carol did their best to perform a delicate political balancing act that they hoped would keep both Hitler and Stalin away from oil-rich Romania. It was an impossible task that ended in 1940 as they barely escaped to fascist Spain and later as they barely escaped to Portugal. They subsequently made it all legal and got married and lived in Cuba, Mexico, Brazil, and Portugal again. He died in 1953; she, in 1977.

And in all that time, do you think they wrote once? Nothing. Not even a postcard, "Having a wonderful time in exile. Regards to all the little Lupescus."

Most of the time I didn't mind, but you'd have thought that on my bar mitzvah, she could have sent a little something. She was, after all, doing a lot better financially than the Lupos. When she moved, it was from, say, Mexico to Brazil. When my father's family moved, which was often, it was from Revere to Dorchester. Romanians move a lot. Some tend to make classier moves than others.

Now Michael, son of the late Carol, says he is willing to

move back to resume the throne in Romania, where he was king twice. The first time, he was only six years old; the pols who helped engineer his father into temporary exile placed the kid on the throne. The second time, he was an adult, but the communists invited him out in 1947. You would think he would have concluded that being king of Romania is not a very steady job.

I certainly have concluded this. I also am concluding that the Romanians have not suffered as they have all these years for a constitutional monarchy. I believe democracy is the operative goal here.

I don't know much about being a king. In my own home, for example, I am seen more as a serf. But I do know something about this democracy business inasmuch as I have covered pols for three decades and once tempted political history by almost losing a Winthrop Town Meeting member race to blanks and vacancies. So I would be happy to travel to Romania as a consultant to maybe someone who would like to become Moldavian county commissioner or a ward alderman out of Bucharest.

But the real reason I do not wish to be king rests in the history of Romania. The original Romanians were the descendants of Roman legions dispatched by the emperor, Trajan. Let Michael settle for king if he wants; I am holding out for emperor.

Kasha *Varnishkes*
à la Academy of Holy Names

There are certain things you do not do in this world.

You do not just suddenly walk into a bikey club and challenge those present to a brawl.

You do not sing "Yankee Doodle" in Tehran.

You do not stay home for dinner if a parochial school graduate cooks kasha *varnishkes.*

Kasha *varnishkes* are essentially groats with noodles. If you don't cook the stuff correctly, you end up with either homemade plaster, handy for improvements to living room or den, or very loose and dry foodstuff that horses might eat if they were on their last hooves.

Something between jellyfish and dust is what's called for in this Jewish dish. The cook in question had a Catholic father and a Lutheran mother.

When it came to steaks, you couldn't ask for better in-laws. Their steaks were thick and juicy and bore no resemblance to the stuff your relatives used to broil to death.

But these same people also ate stuff like macaroni and cheese or spaghetti noodles with canned sauce. Their daughter, a reflection of her times and upbringing, once went into a New York City deli and ordered a corned beef on white with mayo and a glass of milk. The waiter, barely heeding her presence, looked at you and practically ordered you out of both your race and, as they say politely these days, religious persuasion.

So it wasn't as if there hadn't been warnings.

She had converted from a macaroni-and-cheese slave to an inventor of spicy, saucy dishes—Mexican chicken, French chicken, some kind of fancy veal stuff, meatloaf cooked with salad dressing, beef cubes cooked with three different kinds of booze.

None of this indicated she was ready for kasha *var-*

nishkes. Had she not, for example, managed to turn an attempted turkey soup into a pot full of very hot water in which turkey guts were floating like survivors off a wrecked ship?

You would have tried it yourself, but she reminded you of the time you and a pal had promised homemade Chinese food, which turned out to be a large pot of canned brown gravy, on the bottom of which rested in peace a few inedible chunks of cheap beef and some crunchy water chestnuts.

You also were the person who once bought a chuck steak and proceeded to broil it, because, after all, the second operative word was "steak." After two hours of broiling, you noted little progress and still needed a consultant, the landlord's wife, to inform you that chuck steak was beef to be roasted, or, perhaps, avoided altogether.

You and she hardly cook anything anymore anyway because neither son nor daughter has shown any enthusiasm in the last seven years for anything the two of you might cook. Well, almost no enthusiasm.

The son does like a round roast going down for the third time in a sea of gravy; the daughter won't even sit near it. The daughter doesn't like the way calves are bred for veal and refuses, therefore, to eat it; the son doesn't care how they're bred but hates veal anyway. The daughter occasionally will eat some form of chicken; the son avoids most chicken.

So, it was without warning one evening that she announced she was making kasha *varnishkes.* Nobody had asked for them, and you cannot even remember the main dish that they were to accompany. She did indeed produce a pot of groats and a big bowl of noodles. One could indeed mix together the groats and noodles. They were not sopping wet; on the other hand, they were not wet at all.

The son rejected them out of hand. The daughter gave them a shot but was reduced to moving them from one side of the plate to another in an attempt to look busy and not hurt her mother's feelings. You thanked the Academy of the Holy Names alumna for trying this wonderful surprise, but you couldn't bring yourself to finish them. The cook bravely ate her creation, which she insisted was quite good and just needed a little salt, pepper, gravy, booze, blood transfusion or whatever else might be handy.

A good bit of it was left over. It was suggested that people in the sub-Sahara would easily and in good conscience reject what was left over, but that didn't get a big laugh from the cook. An offer to pack it in feed bags and take it to Suffolk Downs brought no yuks at all.

It was given a proper burial in the garbage disposal, over which you silently prayed, "Lord, if you think matzo, the bread of affliction, is a punishment, take a taste of this."

At issue here is not the culinary ability of said wife. There's just something about Jewish food that brings out in her an ever so subtle Torquemada streak. She did a brisket once that melted in one's mouth and tasted of the French wine country. It's supposed to be hard and taste Jewish, but there you are.

Maybe it just proves that in the wide range of ethnic cooking, some morsels resist the American melting pot.

A Couple of Shots of Blended

It may be that Dr. Robert Kohn and Dr. Itzak Levav never dropped in at the Parker House in the 1950s, when hordes of Jewish males, engaged in selling clothing to often recalcitrant retailers, would re-create the wild abandon of Prohibition and seriously test the theory that Jewish guys don't drink.

A recent story by the Associated Press noted, "Jewish men show sharply higher rates of depression than non-Jewish men do, and it may be because they are less likely to drown their sorrows in alcohol . . ."

Two Brown University gentlemen, Kohn and Levav, analyzing surveys in Los Angeles and New Haven, found that in a one-year period, 13 percent of Jewish guys experienced major depression, compared with only 5.4 percent of non-Jewish guys. In speculating as to why, the researchers thought it might have something to do with the low rate of alcoholism among Jewish men—2.8 percent, compared with 14 percent for non-Jewish men.

I don't know. I can drink and be depressed with the best of them, and I've been Jewish since 1938, when I was born in Roxbury. And when my son was born, my father and I went to a synagogue to give him a Hebrew name, got properly happy on a couple of shots of blended, and left with a greater understanding of why some old-timers choose to be devout early in the morning.

Now, I am not making fun of the devout nor am I making little of the diseases of alcoholism and depression. But the study conflicts with Dr. Lupo's totally anecdotal research. Here, then, are some of my findings:

Boston's Jewish salesmen were either giddy or depressed. If business was really very good, they were giddy and often celebrated that by having a couple of shots of Scotch, bourbon, or blended. If business was normal,

111

which they used to describe as, "lousy," or worse, which they used to describe as, "Don't ask," they could be depressed and dealt with that by having a couple of shots of the aforementioned remedies.

When my maternal grandmother walked into the bathroom of her Roxbury apartment, she was surprised to see that the tub was filled with ice and booze. Her daughter's new husband and his friends, including some men of Gaelic persuasion, were celebrating the nuptials. This does not mean, however, that Jewish, or, for that matter, Irish, males drink and bathe at the same time.

My father's father, like many an entrepreneur during Prohibition, made bathtub gin and sold same in little bottles that he kept in the inside pockets of a specially made coat. He was a garment cutter by trade, which probably accounts for his agility with the coat. When he was sufficiently depressed, he left Boston for New York, where his sons found him, drinking Romanian white wine at a Lower East Side cafe. None of this proves anything, but it is a nice story and, so, is included in my research.

In my wild youth, I was known to tipple, as did others. I would never drive and drink. I would just knock down what I thought I could hold and then fall onto the floor. I did much of this in a predominantly Jewish fraternity. I had lots of company. The worst experience followed an evening of drinking Manischewitz red wine. But I learned from experience. From then on, whenever I was invited to a party, I would bring my bottle of Manischewitz which nobody would drink, but I would drink their stuff and still have my bottle to take with me for months to come. I do not recall being depressed while drinking. Indeed, I cannot recall anything. From this you can deduce that most young men of various ethnic backgrounds behave like morons.

On more than one occasion, in places like Doyle's in Jamaica Plain, my Irish friends have insisted that when it comes to hoisting a couple and being depressed to the point of being guilt-ridden, they are more than a match for my ethnic group. Such conversations generally lead to arguments over which group can get depressed faster. Italians, Poles, African Americans, Hispanics, and others in attendance have generally refrained from this debate and appear to be having a better time. Surely, there is something to be learned here.

The other day, my wife and I were having some white wine with our wedding anniversary lunch at a downtown restaurant. I stopped after one and a half goblets. She kept going. I gave her what I didn't drink. She got that glazed look. I was sober and gleeful. This research shows that Jewish guys still try to take advantage of blondes even after thirty-three years of marriage. To some, that may appear revolting, but it ain't depressing.

CHAPTER FIVE

Hello, God
I Haven't Forgotten You,
Especially as I Age

By now, it will have become evident to the reader that I am not a regular shul-goer. Indeed, some of the deeply religious, some of the fundamentalists among us, would charge that I am not even much of a Jew. Let them bray. I am one, and proud of it.

I attend synagogue rarely. I have developed a very personal relationship with God. I communicate often. Sometimes it is to ask for long lives and good health for our loved ones and many others. I do not forget, however, to utter prayers of thanks, of gratitude for the many blessings we have experienced.

Though I do not show up often at shul, and though I have frankly forgotten too many Hebrew letters, and though I cannot engage in Talmudic conversations, I have never lost my respect for the religion or the institution of the synagogue.

We celebrate Pesach and Chanukah. In our own way, sometimes traditionally and sometimes not, we observe Rosh Hashonah and Yom Kippur. My wife and I light candles and utter memorial prayers for parents and in-laws.

The transfer of Jewish thought and culture to our offspring and their loved ones is still a work in progress. This much we know: they are upstanding, moral, kind, generous, courageous, funny people.

So, it is for them also that I have written these stories, which I hope they will cherish and take to heart.

The Saving of a Shul

It is, gentle reader, with a heavy heart and no small sense of humility that I tell you this story, which, you will soon see, is worthy of a Sholom Aleichem, who, were he not dead, would undoubtedly have taken upon himself this task.

He and other scribes of his ilk would have understood the *mishegas,* the craziness, if you will, of the Vilna Shul story. So it must fall to me, for whom it can at least be said, I am alive, though some editors debate this point.

In the shtetl of Boston, squeezed between the murky waters of the Charles and the *shmutzy* whitecaps of Massachusetts Bay, there is a hill named Beacon. It is one of the three original hills of the village settled by the Puritans, who, true, were not crazy about us Jews, but then again were not crazy about anybody else either. They were blessed with consistency.

Another hill was named Copps and is the final resting place for many early settlers, they should rest in peace as they have so done for many years what with live Italians for neighbors, but now, with gentry, who knows what will be with that neighborhood? The third hill was Fort, which they tore down so they could start practicing for urban renewal.

So, the only hill left on which there are those still living is Beacon, and traditionally those living there live very well thank you.

There are on the hill named Beacon two slopes, one slope for the well-off and another slope that used to be for the not-so-well-off, though in these times, you have to be pretty well-off to buy into the not-so-well off. And on the not-so-well-off slope stands the Vilna Shul, though for how long only God in His/Her infinite wisdom knows.

Such is the setting for this tale of woe and much aggravation, what with an old man left in charge, and lots of lawyers, and a developer who got into trouble, and preservationists, and politicians, and a growing cast of so many that it would make for a Cecil B. De Mille Bible epic.

The shul was built on Phillips Street in 1919 by immigrants from, of course, Vilna, Lithuania, a grand center of Jewish learning, whether you are talking the Bible, socialism, or Zionism. In those days, you did not lack for Jewish people on that side of Beacon Hill or across the street in the West End.

They had there accountants and auctioneers, bookies, bakers, butchers, and boxers. You name it, they had it. Every few buildings was a shul because everybody who came from a different city or town wanted his own shul, and even if they came from the same place, they didn't always see eye to eye, you might say, so one shul would not suffice.

In those days, you might avoid the bill collector or the truant officer, but you could not avoid God.

But things being what they are in America, nothing lasts for long. Some people move, and other people get shoved out. The Vilna Shul fell on hard times until only one old-timer, Mendel Miller, was left, and he tried to sell it and give the proceeds to Israeli charities.

Then the Charles River Park Synagogue, where the West End, of blessed memory, used to be, ran to court, insisting it get proceeds. Then one Moshe Blatt, who calls himself the "journey master," broke into the shul with some followers to use it. And then Miller said a developer was going to buy it for condos and parking, but the developer then got into some trouble. And the court got so confused, it appointed a receiver.

I am getting out of breath. But there's more. The Boston Preservation Alliance and Historic Boston Inc. came with a plan to save the shul as a memorial, a righteous and just act. But the Charles River Park Synagogue and some Jewish leaders with clout began fighting the preservationists. Meanwhile, the only ones making out are the lawyers.

The city Landmarks Commission the other night designated the shul as a cultural landmark, and one hopes the mayor, Raymond ben Flynn, and the City Council of elders will approve. A nonprofit group should raise money, and buy it and keep the upstairs as a center of Jewish study and worship. Jews and Gentiles alike are working together on this. For such a blessing, the departed of Vilna would look kindly upon us all.

No Heat, but Much Light

Yea, the firmament was cold, yet the faithful struggled one by one yesterday on the ice-covered sidewalk in front of the Vilna Shul on Phillips Street, Beacon Hill.

They had gathered to commemorate the signing of a purchase-and-sale agreement with a court receiver, thus enabling the Vilna Center for Jewish Heritage to buy and begin repairing the seventy-three-year-old synagogue as a center of Boston Jewish history and culture.

Truly, it was a time and place for miracles. For indeed there cameth suddenly upon the slipping and struggling faithful a city public works truck—filled not with manna but with sand. And two city workers alighted from the truck and spreadeth sand upon the ice, so that the multitudes—thirty-five persons, not counting media—could walketh into the shul.

How came this miracle to pass, a mayoral aide was asked. "People are calling press conferences all over the city just to see if they can get a sander," he jokethed.

And, surely, no sooner had the sand been spread than a black sedan arrived. And alighting from same came one Thomas Menino.

"How come a truck with sand suddenly showed up?" asked one of the scribes in attendance.

And this man, Menino, stopped, and spread his arms to the heavens and said, "The miracle of the mayor."

And so the mayor entered the sanctuary, which was without heat, and where the celebrants could watch their own breath before their very eyes, and he ascended the *bimeh,* the platform on which the Torah scrolls are unrolled and read, and gave the people a proclamation and promised:

"I pledge my support, anything I can do as mayor of this city," he said. "We'll be on your side."

And the people, they rejoiced, as they prepared to raiseth $1.5 million—the next miracle.

Remembering Nine Good Men,
and One Boy, Who Knew How to Pray

Winter's dusk cloaks me as I plod along the grimy remnants of snow, good urban snow, and it all reminds me of
something, a freeze-frame from the past.

In the winter of 1951 or '52, I was throwing snowballs
with another kid. We were pelting buses as they came by,
good big targets, hard to miss. We were getting in some
good hits, when I spied Pelofsky the Hebrew teacher. Not
only the Hebrew teacher was he, but the very man who
had taught me to read the stuff in time for my bar mitzvah
at the little shul one block away from the snowball launch
area.

The little shul had split off from the big shul. Why? Who
knows why? Maybe some old-timers now can remember.
But I didn't care why then, nor do I now, because I just
think that's the way it's supposed to be.

One man says the word "halibut," and another man answers, "overshoes," so you have already a schism and the
rationale for at least two congregations. It has always been
difficult being Jewish, but boring it has never been.

I was fourteen, and I was worried, because Pelofsky was
seventy-five, and he was, to me, a man of biblical propor-
tion, a bearded man sent by God directly to the first floor
of a two-family house, where he made a few extra dollars
teaching American urchins to read from right to left.

His daughter would cook while he and I would sit at the
kitchen table, the surface gritty with crumbs from challah,
and I'd read one of the old brown books, its binding torn.
I'd sit during those cold, dark winter evenings and read
haltingly, and he'd interrupt occasionally to quietly cor-
rect me on a letter or a sound, or maybe not so quietly if
he was in not such a good mood, or if I kept making the
same mistake. Out on his front porch, the other rookies

waited in the dugout for their turn, sometimes not so quietly, and he would give a yell in their direction.

So, now, here I was, and there he was, heading straight
for me, come to visit retribution on an innocent kid who
had done nothing more than show off his Warren Spahn
windup, albeit with a ball of ice.

"You're bar mitzvahed," he reminded me. I awaited the
speech on the responsibilities of manhood, and how they
mitigated against snowballs. But, no, he was the one
throwing curves that evening in the dusk of my youth.
Come to shul, he said. For my sins? No, for a *minyan.* You
need ten men to make a *minyan.* With nine men, God lis-
tens also, but maybe only with one ear. With ten, the party
line is open.

I protested that my mother would worry if I didn't get
home soon. He smiled and told me I'd be home soon
enough. I wouldn't be, as it turned out, because, boy,
those old-timers could pray.

I knew my Hebrew, and I could move along quietly, but
they really rocked. They had been at it a long time. They
knew the territory. One was in his nineties, a man born
before our Civil War.

All were from the old country, from ghettos and shtetls
of which I knew very little. They prayed in Hebrew, but
they conversed and socialized and argued in Yiddish. As
dusk turned officially to evening and headed for night, I
sat, worrying that I was a bush leaguer playing in the
majors.

Then, Pelofsky was at center stage. He was sermonizing,
in Yiddish. He was performing. He'd shake a fist and turn
from side to side. The guy was good, and, hey, he was my
Hebrew teacher, and I was proud.

I had no idea what he was saying. It could have been a
lecture on the building fund, a tirade against anti-Semites,
an impassioned patriotic call to arms for Israel, a social-
ist exhortation.

We Jews don't talk much in Yiddish anymore. The beautifully guttural words linger in the dim memories of narrow streets and triple-deckers, of fire escapes, trash-strewn alleys, and penny candy.

The men wound down finally, a rush of relief, another end to another day of survival, another night of what to them was familiar liturgy and custom and what to me was a foreign, romantic call from other times in other lands. They were nice men who had come from tough times. They were survivors, but they didn't know how to talk easily to fourteen-year-old snowball throwers, and I didn't know enough to talk enough with them.

So, in these times, as dusk turns to evening and heads for night, as I walk through the sooty remnants of snow, I realize I am probably the only survivor of that particular night, yet I cannot tell their story, except to note that they cared very much for what they believed.

Their caring was infectious. When I ran down the street to get home, I was certainly not born-again. But I was not quite the same kid either. They had touched my soul, the old-timers and the little blockhouse stone shul flanked by narrow alleys.

I hope God made a nice place for them. They would be very much surprised to think that I carry them with me, and that the memory warms the winter nights of middle age.

Praying for Compassion

It is a melancholy time, this time of Rosh Hashonah, the Jewish new year, and Yom Kippur, the day of atonement. You remember others, of your own and older generations, who have died. You take a walk or say a prayer, but neither the physical nor emotional exercise overcomes the sadness of the season.

In the soul of memory and mind, you hear the echoes of the shofar, blown in long-abandoned shuls in old city neighborhoods. You hear the heart-wrenching chords of Kol Nidre sung by cantors, older, big men, wearing imposing robes and commanding choirs of other men drawn on this day from the toils of tailoring, teaching, pressing, plumbing, peddling.

You were for too long too immature to believe rabbis who sermonized that such a time as this was good for reflection. It is indeed the best time for that, particularly now in these days of distrust, fear, and selfishness.

You recall that the rabbi would offer a prayer for the government, would ask God to guide politicians in wisdom and compassion. You wonder now if some astute rabbi will pray for the continued existence of government, period, end of prayer. Wisdom and compassion took a holiday long before Rosh Hashonah and will not be back anytime soon after Yom Kippur.

Those who oppose taxes, those who will vote against their own best interests in favor of a tax rollback, swear up and down that they are not selfish. They are financially strapped, they insist, and maybe even afraid. They say they can't take it anymore. They have convinced themselves that all they need do is make a clean sweep of all politicians and the new taxes, and, somehow, all will be well again.

Logic means nothing. Facts will not stand in their way.

Anecdotes raised to counter their own examples are pushed aside as exceptions to what they insist is the rule. And compassion? That is given lip service. When mourning this season those who have passed on, you mourn also the death of compassion.

There is no claim here that the Jewish concepts of charity and compassion are any better or worse than those put forth by the Christian, the Muslim, the Hindu, the Buddhist, or the morally driven atheist or agnostic. Nor do you suggest that you have any monopoly on such concepts or how they are supposed to operate.

But this much you know. To be charitable and compassionate in good times doesn't take much. To be so in bad times is when it counts. These are indeed economically bad times, but they are far from the worst of times. You can remember times much worse, and you know in your gut that should compassion dry up like a prune, the times will indeed get worse.

During every holiday in every religion, the clergy tell familiar stories that the congregants have heard before, stories of faith, or hope, or redemption. You are no wise man, but have an old story, one you have told before, in speech and in print. It bears telling again.

Your mother's mother was a generous woman, a Russian Jew who lived in a Chelsea tenement with three daughters and a son. She cooked, sewed, cleaned, mothered, and ran a dry goods store nearby. She got up early in the darkened morning before the kids and retired early the next morning long after they went to bed.

Your mother remembered how beggars would come to the store or even the apartment and ask for a penny. Your grandmother would give a penny to each one. The kids, noting they were not yet the Rockefellers, asked her why, asked her how could she know the beggars needed the money.

Well, she answered, nine of ten may not, but how would she feel if she refused the one who did?

Indeed, there is waste, and there is corruption. But there are also the thousands of good people serving thousands of others who need help. In this time, when we are reminded of the virtue of compassion, shall we withhold the inflated pennies?

Or should each of us remember not even the Hebrew words or prophets, but the guttural Yiddish of immigrants who loved America and gave of themselves:

Zei a menich. Be a mensch.

SOURCES AND ACKNOWLEDGMENTS

The Boston Globe, reprinted with permission
"Acting to Make Parents Proud" (8/10/94)
"Ahead of Her Time for Going On-Line" (8/13/96)
"A Bad Bet" (6/22/93)
"Comforting New Generations" (12/15/96)
"The Continuity of Family" (9/26/92)
"A Couple of Shots of Blended" (6/11/98)
"Diversity: So What's the Problem?" (7/9/95)
"From Russia with Hate" (12/20/93)
"Grandma's Favorite Warning" (8/23/96)
"A House and Its Memories" (3/1/91)
"Is There a Double Standard for Jews?" (4/23/88)
"The Jewish Defense League" (1/18/70)
"Kasha *Varnishkes* à la Academy of Holy Names" (8/16/89)
"Memories of Max" (1/26/91)
"My Son the Cop" (2/9/94)
"Noblesse Obliges Him to Forgo the Throne" (12/30/89)
"No Heat, but Much Light" (1/21/94)
"On Christmas Eve, a Toast to Two Who Cared" (12/24/88)
"Praying for Compassion" (9/22/90)
"Remembering Nine Good Men, and One Boy, Who Knew How
    to Pray" (2/28/87)
"The Saving of a Shul" (12/16/89)
"Sticking by the Union" (9/3/95)
"A Stroll through the Old Neighborhood" (9/3/88)
"Thanks, but It's Too Late" (7/10/93)
"Those Who Judge Israel" (11/10/90)
"Where a Sigh Can Speak Volumes" (4/16/95)

Boston Magazine, reprinted with permission
"The Messiah Comes Tomorrow" (11/73)

The Middletown [N.Y.] Times-Herald Record, reprinted
with permission
"Drucker, Murder, Inc., Hoodlum, Dies in Prison" (1/24/62)

The Baltimore Evening Sun
    "Burlesque Comedian Reminisces about Early Days—and the
        Changes"
    "Used Clothing Store Brings 'Block' Madison Ave. Pitch"
        (6/24/64)

This Week: Supplement to *Brookline Citizen, Allston Brighton Citizen-Item, Boston Ledger*
    "Today I Am a Fountain Penski" (9/85)

Thanks to Paul Wright of the University of Massachusetts
Press, *Globe* librarian Liz Donovan, *Globe* technical wizard
Sean Mullin, and my *Globe* editors Wendy Fox and Ellen
Clegg—for putting up with my kvetching.

Alan Lupo, an author and veteran journalist, has spent many years covering the personalities and issues of urban America, including racial, ethnic, and class tensions; crime; politics; government; and neighborhood survival. In his forty-year career, he has been a newspaper reporter, columnist, television anchor and reporter, magazine writer and editor, radio commentator, and a teacher and lecturer at various universities. *The Messiah Comes Tomorrow* is his fourth book. He lives with his wife, Caryl Rivers, an author, journalist, and professor, in Winthrop, Massachusetts. Lupo is a staff writer for the *Boston Globe*.